Published by Eagle Publications
P O Box 73374, London W3 3FZ, England.
A Paperback Original

First published in the United Kingdom in 2019

Text copyright © 2019 Roselle Thompson

The right of Roselle Thompson to be identified as the Author
of this work has been asserted by her.

Cover design by V3Creative Designs

ISBN 978-0-952325-9-7

A CIP catalogue record for this book is available from the British Library
All Rights Reserved
This book is sold subject to the condition that it shall not, by way of trade or otherwise, be lent, hired out or otherwise circulated in any form of binding or cover other than that in which it is published. No part of this publication may be reproduced, stored in a retrieval system, or transmitted in any form or by any means (electronic, mechanical, photocopying, recording or otherwise) without the prior written permission of Eagle Publications.

All paper used by Eagle Publications is SFI (Sustainable Forestry Initiative) and PEFC (Programme for the Endorsement of Forest Certification Schemes) Certified.
This is a work of fiction. Names, characters, incidents and dialogues are products of the author's imagination or are used fictitiously. Any resemblance to actual people, living or dead, events or locales is entirely coincidental.

Printed in the United Kingdom and United States by
Lightning Source for Eagle Publishers

www.eaglepublications.co.uk

EAGLE PUBLICATIONS

Who is this book for?
Phoenix Study Guides aim to give you the highest quality books to strengthen pupils' Foundation English. They provide the facts and rules needed to help them understand English correctly. This lets them experience how easy reading and writing skills can be developed, once the rules are known. A child's progress in each unit can be assessed by the Exercises presented at the end of each section.
This book is designed for three groups of students. The first group is the 7 to 12 year olds, who are working towards Key Stage 2 SATs Assessment Tests in Year 6. If you are in this group, then you are at the end of your Primary School stage, and are about to start Secondary School.

The second group is made up of students who are preparing for 11+ exams for independent and grammar schools. This book provides a comprehensive course in spelling, and vocabulary development at this stage; together with comprehension and word-power development skills, needed for both verbal reasoning and creative writing.
The third group is made up of 7 to 12 year olds, who work independently at home or in school. All of the books in this series are free-standing, so a child can work through each of them or focus on the individual subject needs of the child. Whichever group you belong to, your confidence and competence will grow, as you practice and improve your knowledge for life with these exercises. As your knowledge of English vocabulary expands, you will be excited and motivated by your developing skills and improved performance, not only in school but in life generally.

About This Book
This book **supports the whole of the Key Stage 2 & 3 English curriculum** for success in responding to texts and the writers' perspectives. It will help you to develop your Comprehension skills so that you can be successful in learning English. You will not only learn new words and build your vocabulary and grammar thoroughly, but you will also be motivated to extend your understanding and demonstrate this in both school work and exams.

Teachers will find this book useful as the passages here can either be used in group work or for individual learners to use at their own pace in the classroom and for extended work at home. This book therefore has a dual purpose – it not only teaches but also tests students' overall mastery of their comprehension as they develop. Also included in this book is your reward, a *Certificate of Achievement*, which marks your successful completion of this book. An **Answer key** for the questions of each passage is at the back of the book. **There are also Writing Tasks at the end of each passage** to help consolidate reading, and comprehension skills, with your own writing.

Other books in this Series are:
- *English Grammar: A Student's Companion*
- *Spelling & Word-Power Skills*
- *11+ English Preparation Tests for the CEM*
- *Vocabulary Skills for Students & Teachers -- Volumes 1 & 2*

How the book is organized
This book provides a complete package of introduction, revision and practice comprehension passages to help you with preparation for the Key Stage SATSs tests and those preparing for the 11+ independent and State Grammar School, Common Entrance exams at 13+ and preparation for GCSE English Language Paper 1. The passages cover work in Key Stage Two and Three, of the National Curriculum and beyond. **The texts in this book have been carefully selected to be age-appropriate and cover a range of text types.** The format of the questions replicates the Reading and Comprehension components of the tests to help your child become familiar with the exam format and requirements. A *Certificate of Achievement* is provided at the end of the book to give you a sense of reward for your hard work in completing the book.

The right of Roselle Thompson to be identified as the author of this work has been asserted by her in accordance with the Copyright, Designs & Patents Act 1988. All rights reserved. No part of this publication may be reproduced in any material form (including photocopying or storing it in any medium by electronic means and whether or not transiently or incidentally to some other use of this publication), without the written permission of the copyright owner, except in accordance with the provisions of the Copyright, Designs and Patents Act 1988. Applications for the copyright owner's written permission to reproduce any part of this publication should be addressed to the publisher – *Eagle Publications*. British Library Cataloguing in Publication Data. A CIP record of this book is available from the British Library. **Warning:** The doing of an unauthorized act in relation to this copyright work may result in court action as a claim for damages and criminal prosecution.

Published in the UK: Eagle Publications, P O Box 73374, London W3 3FZ, UK
Email: eaglepublications58@gmail.com   www.eaglepublications.co.uk
Enquiries: 07739655603/07848 844 377   ISBN 978-9542325-9-7

Phoenix Study Guides

MASTERING COMPREHENSION SKILLS

Essential for SATS, 11+ & 13+ EXAMS

By

Roselle Thompson

This book belongs to:

Name……………………………………………………………

CONTENTS PAGE

	Texts	Type of Text	Page
1.	The Hunter and the White Bear	Fiction - Narrative	1
2.	Spice Island Beauty	Fiction Recount	5
3.	Pandas	Non-fiction - Information	7
4.	The Wilkinson Family	Fiction - Narrative	10
5.	Camping & the Great Outdoors	Non-fiction - Information	12
6.	Queen Bess – An Inspiration	Non-fiction - Biography	15
7.	Bath Town: a British Heritage	Non-fiction - Factual	20
8.	Homework Blues	Fiction - Narrative	23
9.	Man Walks on the Moon	Non-Fiction - Factual	26
10.	The Fugitive	Fiction - Narrative	30
11.	Forests in Crisis	Non-fiction - Information	33
12.	A Farewell into the Unknown	Fiction - Narrative	36
13.	Letter Writing	Persuasive Narrative	40
14.	Ode to Seasons in the Tropics	Power of Imagery	42
15.	Holiday Villa for Rent	Non-Fiction - Advertisement	44
16.	**WRITING TASKS:** A List of Writing Tasks		46
17.	**Answers to Passages in this Book**		47
18.	**About the Author & Other Books in the Series**		57

COMPREHENSION – SOURCES OF ANSWERS

What is comprehension? Why is it important to you? Firstly, the origin of the word comes from Latin *comprehensionem*; as well as Middle French *comprehendere* and both sources mean *"to understand."* Comprehension is the ability to process information from a text, understand its meaning and show your actual understanding of the text by responding to it. When you are unable to comprehend or understand a difficult word, you would normally look it up its meaning in a dictionary. That is why when pupils do comprehension; they do an exercise to find out how well they understand the written (or spoken) text.

Here is a careful selection of mixed genre texts, which demonstrate major genre types from fiction, fact to advertisement. They will help you develop your reading skills so that you can understand and enjoy what you read. In addition, they will stretch and extend your general understanding of different types of reading materials, as you explore the writer's perspectives in each passage.

Comprehension question types in this book fall into four main types

Type	Where/how to find the answer	Example
Factual content/Literal	Specifically stated in text	Gives a text that explains you might be asked how a person was at the time of her accident. The answer will be specifically stated in the text.
Logical sequence & Inference	Not directly stated in text but can be inferred (understood) from the details given	Gives a text that describes a setting on a cold snow and dark night. You may be asked what season it is in the story or to identify True or False Statements. You must use the hints given in the passage to work out the most likely answer.
Personal judgment/Prediction	Not directly stated in the text but you must read more deeply into the text to form your own opinion	You may be asked to describe the feelings or reactions of a character or about the intentions of the author e.g. what was Tom's mood on his first day at school? You must read between the lines and look at the language and tone used to form your own opinion.
Knowledge of grammar, vocabulary and literary techniques & Evaluation	Not stated in the text at all but you must use your knowledge to answer the question	Questions may ask you about words meaning or ask you to recognize literary techniques such as alliteration, onomatopoeia, simile, metaphor. Be careful with vocabulary questions. Answer options may provide a correct definition of a work but only one will fit the context of the passage.

FOR EXAMPLE:
- Knowledge of **literary techniques** requirements – e.g. alliteration/metaphor
- Readers **personal judgment** requires – reference to text within the context of the passage
- References to lines in the text
- Readers logical **inference** requirement – refer to text as a whole to make decisions
- Knowledge of **vocabulary** requirement
- Knowledge of **grammar** – the tense of a sentence/prepositions, conjunction

There are also **Writing Tasks at the end of each Comprehension passage**, to help consolidate your knowledge and understanding of the texts. Therefore, by linking the skills learnt, you can then create your own texts from the tasks.

THE HUNTER & THE WHITE BEAR

Many years ago, deep in the middle of the densest forest, a brave hunter from an African village caught the rarest and most unique animal anyone had ever seen. It was a giant white bear with soft pink eyes; known for giving good luck and supernatural powers to anyone who caught it and kept it safely. The bear was beautiful to look at. Weighing about 700kg, it was a huge mass of soft, white, fluffy fur. Its legs were stocky, with small ears and a stubbly tail. However, its feet were very large with short, sharp claws. Everyone marvelled at the existence of the white bear.

Long before this amazing feat, the older generation of the village had told tales about this great magical white bear, which most people believed existed and wished they could catch because of the fame and fortune it would bring them. However, no one had ever seen a white bear. Brown African bears were common but they provided no great challenge to catch, as this white one did. Furthermore, because no one had seen a white bear, most of the young people of this village had dismissed the story about the white mystical bear, saying that it was just a superstitious tale.

What was remarkable about this brave hunter is that he decided to take the bear back to his village to prove that he was an awesome hunter, the best in the land and most important, to claim the fame and fortune that is so well-known about this magical animal. The hunter was a poor man, with a large family who needed many things, food, clothing, a better home, as their roof leaked and money too. He thought of all the things a small fortune could help him to buy, to make his life more comfortable and this made him feel excited but at the same time, nervous with enthusiasm. He was the luckiest man in the whole world, he thought.

But after falling asleep whilst thinking about his good luck, he woke up in the morning with the bear lying a little distance from him, he took a long hard look at the amazing animal and then an idea came to him. He was a generous person, and knowing that his family would be well taken care of, he thought, "I will give this beautiful animal to my king as a gift." So he set off on a long journey to the king's palace, with the animal walking obediently alongside him. They had walked for miles when the hunter became tired and very hungry. He stopped at a wooden cottage, where he hoped he could get some water to drink and food to eat. When he knocked on the door, a man's scary voice inside yelled out to him, "You are here too early! I am not ready for you yet, go away and come back later!" the voice ordered.

The hunter was surprised, as he had no idea what the man was talking about, so he kept knocking on the cottage door. The man inside became more irritated and began to sound annoyed.

"I told you to go away!" he yelled out boldly, "I'm not ready for you yet!"

The hunter was quite puzzled. He scratched his head and looked around him trying to make sense of what was happening. The man inside the cottage shouted, "I need a few more hours. I've only prepared half the delicious food. Please, I need more time!"

At this point with the mention of the words "*delicious food*", the hunter was starving. It was clear that there must be some mistake so he shrugged his shoulders and knocked again. This time the man swung opened the door in frustration and anger, ready to yell at his expected visitors. He was just about to yell some more but instantly relaxed when he saw the hunter and the white bear standing at his door.

"Oh- -oh, it's you!" He said in surprise. I was expecting some nasty trolls, who have been here with threats that I either prepare food for them or they would kill me," said the anxious man, somewhat relieved that it was a hunter and not the nasty trolls.

"How can I help you?" asked the man.

The hunter asked if he and the white bear could eat and rest for a while before continuing on their journey. The man glanced nervously around, and then whispered, "I would like to help you but I can't. You see, many fierce trolls are planning to come down from the mountains to my home tonight. If I feed you and your bear I will have no food for them, they will harm me."

It was obvious from the amount of food that had been laid on the table that the man had been cooking for hours. Every space on the man's immense table was filled with a wonderful feast, and it made the hunter's stomach growl with hunger even more.

"Look we won't eat everything, the hunter said, reassuring him, "Just enough to stop our hunger pains, we'll soon be on a way again."

"You don't know those nasty troll, the man explained," in a high-pitched voice, sounding desperate with fear.

"Give us some food, and I will help you with the trolls," the hunter said.

The man was not sure what he should do. He could really do with the help for sure, but he knew those nasty trolls; they were mean and vicious and never listened to anyone. Deep in thought, he pursed his lips. Then pinching his chin with his fingers, he lightly tapped his upper lip for a moment, then came up with some ideas.

"I will scare the trolls away because I am a brave hunter," the hunter announced boldly, "Let me stay and help you."

"Very well," said the man who was tired of cooking for the trolls, "Come in and have some food. Then give some to your ghostly looking animal over there," he said, pointing to the white magical bear with pink eyes. Later, I will leave my house to you, so you can deal with those nasty trolls."

"Alright," said the Hunter, "I have a brilliant idea."

The Hunter knew that he had to come up with a brilliant plan so he wouldn't let the man down. At the same time he knew that the trolls were many but he was only one person - an uneven match! He left the man's house and sat under a tree at the back of the house, while he surveyed the surroundings, looking for the best possible ideas as to how he was going to defeat the trolls.

In the meantime the man, who was sitting inside the house, was nervous. He knew that these nasty trolls were vicious and he doubted the Hunter could get rid of them, but he was willing to give the Hunter a chance. He paced noisily up and down in his room, because he found it difficult to sit still. During some moments of thinking about his predicament, the man felt this Hunter, who was obviously brave, as he had caught a white bear, probably stood a good chance of getting rid of the nasty trolls. The man rubbed his hands together in glee; already imagining the excitement of the Hunter's victory.

However, the more he thought about the situation and how fierce the nasty trolls were; he would change his expression and become fearful with a frown. At times feeling afraid, he would nervously look out of his window, in case the trolls were near. Other times, with his hands behind his back and his head hung down, he would pace up and down his room, biting his lips, and worried that he could be in greater danger, if the Hunter lost this battle with the trolls. But he thought of how often he had experienced the terror of the trolls and how miserable his life had become, with their threatening demands. He wanted the Hunter to defeat the trolls.

"Ok, I've got it!" said the Hunter to himself, entering the house to tell the man about his plan.

The next day, the man was happy to make the most delicious meal. You could smell the aroma from a great distance. In fact, he was sure the nasty trolls would smell the delicious food and prepare to attack once more. Both men ate and were happy with the plan to defeat the trolls. It was not long before, they had eaten there was a knock on the door. The nasty trolls were back again, thinking they would terrify the poor man once more.

They stood outside the door, with their horrible angry faces, their huge eyes and tongues hanging down, ready to charge into the man's house.   Then they knocked. There was not a sound from inside the house. They knocked again, this time harder than the first time, and no one came to the door. They could smell the delicious food that was inside and their mouths were full of saliva, ready to gobble up the food and maybe the man, so they became impatient with their knocking. There was still not a single sound from inside the house. The nasty trolls were used to getting an immediate answer, from the terrified man but this time it was different, so they became more angry that they were kept waiting.

(c) 2019 Roselle Thompson *Mastering Comprehension Skills*

They hopped and jumped and made angry howling noises outside the door, as trolls do, preparing to charge into the man's house, to gobble him up and eat whatever food they could find. Their noises became louder and they became more hungry and angry, so they charged into the man's house. Through the broken front door, they charged only to find that a huge strong net from the ceiling had dropped firmly on them. They struggled to free themselves but the Hunter's white bear, which was waiting for them inside the house, growled angrily and loudly at them. His pink eyes flashed at them and it charged towards the trapped trolls.

The white bear was so terrifying to the trolls they felt certain that it would eat them up. So they begged to be set free.

"Please don't eat us!" they yelled. "We promise we will not hurt anyone and will never come back here again!"

The white bear growled even louder, flashing his white teeth and his pink magical eyes glistened and glowed like fire. The trolls were huddled together inside the trap, frightened of the immense animal, as they trembled with fear. During this great moment of defeat, the man and the Hunter, who were both hiding in the other room, listening to the trolls begging for mercy, were ecstatic with happiness. At last, they had conquered the nasty trolls, and were relieved that would never see them again.

QUESTIONS

1. What was thought to be special about the white bear?
2. Describe most people's reaction to the tale, and explain why they behaved this way?
3. How would anyone benefit from catching the white bear?
4. What did the hunter want to prove by taking the white bear home?
5. List at least 4 things that the hunter and his family could do with his prize money.
6. Which word in *paragraph 4* tells us that the hunter is not a greedy or selfish person?
7. What was the hunter's plan when he got back home to his family?
8. Why did the hunter stop at the cottage?
9. How did the hunter react to the answer he got, when he knocked on the cottage door?
10. What does the reply from the man in the cottage tell us about his general experience?
11. How would you describe the tone of voice of the man in the cottage?
12. Why was there a doubt as to whether the Hunter would succeed in getting rid of the trolls?
13. In *paragraph 2* which word means *"excitement"*?
14. Describe the man's fearful behaviour.
15. From *paragraph 5*, find the word describes the *smell of food or drink*?
16. What made the trolls impatient once they had knocked on the cottage door?
17. Describe how the trolls were defeated?
18. What is the meaning of the word *"predicament"* in paragraph 3?
    a. From *paragraph 8*, list at least 12 verbs.
    b. What effect do these verbs have in the paragraph?
19. Why was it important to defeat the trolls at this stage?
20. How would you describe the ending of the story?

WRITING TASK:

Write <u>an imaginative story</u> entitled: *"They Came at Midnight!"*

SPICE ISLAND BEAUTY

It was already 5.30pm when we left the carénage[1], in St. George's lively waterfront promenade, which winds around the town's inner harbour; a place of unrivalled natural beauty. This horseshoe-shaped promenade was indeed a joy to behold. Hugging the harbour is an array of colourful hillside buildings that stand tall in a staggered arrangement; as if on parade. They form a natural amphitheatre around the shimmering blue sea water; all which are further surrounded by mountainous heights in the distance beyond.

We viewed each part of the curved harbour from every vantage point across the water. This was filled with boats either bobbing at their moorings or slowing gliding backwards and forwards across the blue expanse. A foreign cruise ship, which dominated a part of the view where it was moored, was a giant among the many smaller, local, colourful, wooden boats.

We spent half a day, strolling along the water's edge, taking in the hustle and bustle of people moving to and fro with supplies, as they loaded boats. These beautifully crafted wooden boats, brightly painted in a feast of primary colours; red, yellow, orange, green and blue, are used for trading goods among neighbouring islands. Many of them are built on the beach from a mixture of a local wood known as white cedar, for the frames, and imported greenheart wood, for the keels. We were told that the elegant and graceful curves which are characteristics of these lovely crafted boats are made by local builders who often do not use instruments, but build the boats to their own personal specifications and tastes! Falling captivated by the mesmerising effect of this beautiful landscape, we basked in this prime focus of natural and unequalled beauty, before resigning ourselves to the sumptuous tastes of tropical cuisine, at the end of the day.

By 6.30pm we left the town and headed for our hotel, which was located in the northern part of the small island. We accepted the long journey ahead of us with quiet resignation, since we had specifically chosen the quietness of the rural countryside for our summer holiday abroad, instead of the busy town. Glen, our local driver, knew the roads well; especially where to avoid the ruts as he careered around bends in the night air. Travelling quickly, from the main town, across another – Grenville, the second largest town in the island, it soon became almost completely dark. Night had fallen fast and there was hardly anyone in sight on the lonely winding roads ahead. Giant trees flanked the narrow roads, and the night sounds of the braying donkeys and the barking of dogs intermittently around us, could be heard in the distance.

By good fortune, after an interminable and exhausting ride back to our hotel, our driver finally stopped at the entrance. We disembarked quietly and ambled into the hotel reception; tired from a long day and the hasty journey, straight to our rooms. We were delighted at our safe return, and grateful for the indelible memories we now shared - a great and unforgettable day in Grenada.

Glossary
[1] *The French name is derived from the practice of turning a ship on its side for cleaning or repairing below the water line; a practice which had been done in this area in Grenada for many years.*

QUESTIONS

1. What word in *paragraph 1* describes the appearance of the promenade?
2. What is the narrator's opinion of the Carenage? Support your answer with evidence from the text.
3. Which word personifies how the houses behave in *paragraph 1*?
4. What does the word "amphitheatre" mean in the context of the passage?
5. Give 2 verbs which describe the movement of the boats on the sea water.
6. What literary device describes the foreign cruise ship in *paragraph 2*?
7. The cruise ship was "moored" – what does this verb mean?
8. What does the phrase *"hustle and bustle"* suggest about the activity at the Carenage?
9. Which types of wood is used in boat-building at the Carenage?
10. How do we know that greenheart wood is not grown in Grenada?
11. What is interesting about how the local boats are built?
12. Describe in your own words the narrator's experience and feelings of the Carenage, as described in *paragraph 3*.
13. What does the verb "resigning" mean in *paragraph 3*?
14. Why had the narrator chosen to holiday in the countryside instead of the town?
15. How would you describe the condition of the roads during the journey to their hotel?
16. How do we know that Glen the driver was driving fast? Support your answer with evidence from the text.
17. Give evidence of two instances in the text which suggest that the journey to their hotel was very long.
18. (a). What does the word "intermittently" mean?
    (b). What part of speech or word-category is this word?
19. Which words in *paragraph 5* describe the narrator's feelings at the end of the journey?
20. What does the word "indelible" mean?
21. What is the meaning of the phrase *"by good fortune"*?
22. Describe how the buildings around the harbour are presented in the text.
23. What is a promenade and where is one located in this text?
24. What is suggested by the phrase *"the blue expanse"* in the text?
25. In your own words, summarise the narrator's visit to the Carenage in St. Georges, in the text.

WRITING TASK:

Write a Factual Story about an experience that you have had entitled, ***"A Journey I Shall Never Forget!"***

PANDAS

Giant Pandas, popularly called Pandas, live in South-western China's dense bamboo forests which are misty and rainy. These cuddly-looking animals are easily recognised by their white and black fur and black patches on their eyes, are omnivores. They will sometimes eat fish and small animals, but their diet is made up of 99% bamboos leaves from trees that are amongst the longest plants in the world. Pandas like to eat these because they are nice and juicy to eat. Giant Pandas are related to the polar bear, black bear, and grizzly bear which are all carnivores. Although they live in different parts of the world, these animals live in forests but eat different food. Pandas are big eaters and will fill their bellies for up to 12 hours of eating in one day.

Giant pandas grow to between 1.2m and 1.5m, and weigh between 75kg and 150 kg. At the back of its body the panda has a small tail and it also walks on four legs to travel. As for their children, baby pandas are born pink, measuring about 15cm, roughly the size of a small ruler and they only weigh approximately 150 grams at birth. Baby pandas are also born blind and only open their eyes six to eight weeks after birth. However, when they turn into adults they can weigh up to 150 kg. Pandas are fat, and this makes them very good climbers. They have thick fur which protects them from the cold snow.

Pandas are solitary animals. The males and females live separately but occasionally meet outside of breeding season or come together during this season briefly, in order to mate. Research suggests that pandas communicate with each other through scent-marks and distinctive calls. They are one of the world's rarest animals, as they are threatened with extinction. Sadly there are now only approximately 1,500 of these bears surviving in the wild. Scientists are not sure how long pandas live in the wild, but in captivity, they can live up to 30 years.

QUESTIONS

MULTIPLE CHOICE QUESTIONS - *Circle the correct answer – either A, B, C, or D*

1. **Baby pandas are born**
   a. With black and white spots
   b. Pink
   c. White all over
   d. With no fur

2. **Giant pandas live in**
   a. Australia's wood lands
   b. Bamboo forests in Southern China
   c. Florida, safari parks
   d. Large Zoos around the world

3. **Giant pandas eat mainly**
   a. Soft young leaves
   b. Insects
   c. Fruit and grain
   d. Bamboo leaves

4. **The Giant Panda is related to**
   a. Reindeer
   b. Polar and Grizzly bears
   c. Mountain lions
   d. Winnie the Pooh

5. **Tick Only the Statements that are TRUE**

i.	Baby pandas are born blind	
ii.	Baby pandas are over 30cm at birth	
iii.	Pandas eat sweet juicy bamboo leaves	
iv.	Pandas communicate with each other by special calls	
v.	Giant pandas are rare	
vi.	Pandas do not have tails	
vii.	They are threatened with extinction	
viii.	Pandas live in the wild for over 30 years	
ix.	Bamboo plants are among the shortest trees in the world	
x.	Pandas eat fish and also small animals	

6. **Other bears are different from Giant pandas because**
   a. They have less spots
   b. Are larger in size
   c. They are carnivores
   d. Live in the desert

7. **Giant pandas weigh between**
   a. 75 and 100kg
   b. 225 and 500kg
   c. 75 and 150kg
   d. 150 and 750kg

8. **To fill their bellies a Giant panda would eat**
   a. 24 hours in a day

b. 15 hours in a day
c. 60 hours a week
d. 12 hours in a day

9. At birth a Giant panda's baby measures
a. The size of a small shoe
b. The size of a ruler
c. The size of a pair of scissors
d. The size of a stapler

10. When are baby pandas eyes open after they are born?
a. A day after birth
b. 6 weeks after birth
c. A fortnight after birth
d. 10 weeks after birth

11. What does the word "solitary" suggest about pandas in paragraph 3
a. They like being with a crowd of other giant pandas
b. They like walking in pairs
c. They prefer to be alone
d. They are great group hunters

12. Male and female pandas live
a. Together with their young
b. Hunt other animals in packs
c. Live separately, get together to mate
d. Together near to bamboo forests

13. Put a T for TRUE and F for FALSE in the Box

i.	There are over 2500 Giant pandas living	
ii.	Giant Pandas are easily recognized	
iii.	Scientists think that Giant Pandas live for up to 30 years in the wild	
iv.	Pandas are too big and fat to climb	
v.	Pandas walk on 2 legs	
vi.	Pandas have black patches on their eyes	
vii.	Their thick fur protects them from the cold	
viii.	When Baby Pandas become adults they can weigh up to 150kg	
ix.	Pandas communicate well through smelling	
x.	Bamboo forests are often misty and rainy	

14. Pandas are omnivores, which means they
a. Eat fish and meat only
b. Eat both plant and animals
c. Eat only bamboo leaves
d. Eat both grass and leaves

WRITING TASK:

Do some of your own research on Giant Pandas, then **Write a Speech** for your Year Group, about the threat of extinction of Giant Pandas; together with your own suggestions about what could be done to help the situation.

THE WILKINSON FAMILY

The Wilkinsons are a family of five from Brooklyn, New York in America, who now live in England. They have a dog called Rex which is a Labrador. The father who is called Edward and mother who is Josephine have three children. Mel, who is 9 years, is the only girl with two brothers; Reece who is 10 years and Pete who is 5 years old.

Mr. Wilkinson is a GP and many people go to see him when they are sick. Mr. Wilkinson's Surgery is not local, so he has to commute 5 miles into Central London each day. Mrs. Wilkinson is a Dentist who drives to her job. She is a very pleasant person who always smiles when she sees all the clients who come to the Dental Surgery.

Reece, Mel and Pete go to Grange Park Primary School. Grange Park Primary School is a local school near to the Children's home, where they have many friends. Reece and Pete are involved in many activities during the week, such as after-school Film Club, Football, Karate and Swimming. On Tuesdays they go swimming and attend Boys Scout, where they learn different skills such as learning to create interesting paper crafts, tying knots, going on treasure trails and crafty ideas such as making memory boxes. When the weather is good, especially during the summer, their Scout group goes camping. Reece is allowed to go camping with the group, when they put up tents, build campfires and sing lots of new songs. The boys love camping and look forward to their annual activity.

Mel is also busy during the week with lots of her own activities; she goes swimming on Thursdays at the local Leisure Centre, where she is trained in a group of under 10year olds by Bernie, who thinks that Mel is a brilliant swimmer. On Mondays after school, Mel plays volleyball with her best friend Samantha. The girls also have an hour's piano lesson before lunch on Saturdays. After that they enjoy their ballet lesson until 3pm on Saturday mornings. After such a busy day the girls relax in the afternoons.

Saturday afternoon free time is catch-up time for Mel. That's when she makes contact with her old friends from America. She sends texts, and emails or chats on *Whats App* and *Snap chat*. Mel and her friends exchange photos about what they have been doing. Although Mel misses her old friends, she is really enjoying life in England too. She hopes to see some of her old American friends soon and has also promised to take her best English friend Samantha with her, when she visits her grandmother and grandfather, during the summer holidays.

Sunday is family time together – no special activity for anyone. The Wilkinsons just enjoy the day doing whatever pleases them as a family. When they choose to go walking in the park, they often have great times chasing Rex, their Alsatian dog around the park.

QUESTIONS

1. Where are the Wilkinson family from?
2. How many people is the Wilkinson family made up of?
3. What is the name of the children's school?
4. How old are the Wilkinson's family children?
5. What after-school activities do the children do?
6. How many activities does Mel attend in a week?
7. How does Mel stay in touch with their old American friends?
8. What is Mrs Wilkinson job?
9. Who is Mel's swimming teacher and what does she think about Mel's swimming?
10. What are Reece's activities on Tuesdays?
11. What is Reece likely to do during the summer?
12. Who is a GP and what does a GP do?
13. What are some of the things that Mrs Wilkinson is likely to do as a Dentist?
14. What breed of dog is Rex?
15. Who is Samantha, and what does she do during the week?
16. Where is Samantha expected to be during the summer?
17. How many activities is Reece involved in during the week?
18. Name some of the things that Pete does.
19. Where is Brooklyn in America?
20. What activities do you do during your school week? How do they compare with the Wilson children?

WRITING TASK:

Imagine you were Mel; **write a letter** to your old friend in America, telling her about your life in England, since leaving the USA.

CAMPING – ENJOYING THE GREAT OUTDOORS!

Camping is not only for boy Scouts and girl Guides, it can be a great experience for people of all ages. This activity is becoming very popular and there are lots of great campsite locations around the globe where you can enjoy camping. For example, whether you are camping with your friends or family, you will certainly have a great opportunity of living amongst nature and experiencing time away from your everyday homes.

Many campsites nowadays are designed to accommodate almost any request you might have, even catering for your pets! For example, forest camping allows you to choose a designated camping site or you may choose to sample camping in the wild under tents. Tent camping sites often cost less than campsites with full facilities, and most will allow direct access by car.

However, because you are exchanging your comfort zones for sleeping in campsites or camping in the forest, the first thing to realise is that this has its own unique issues and challenges. These can range from questions about how to pitch your tent, how you'll cook your food, whether there are enough activities for children and other concerns that forest campers encounter. Whichever, method of sleeping in the outdoors you choose, you will need to plan well in advance, before packing and organising your camping trip. This is to minimise the likelihood of unhappy experiences, and maximise your enjoyment of your outdoor camping experience. Here are some of the important first steps to consider.

THE TENT
The tent is perhaps the most important item you will need to have for your adventure; especially if you have chosen wild camping. For those who are staying in designated camping site you may have the use of a caravan or campervan or other form of mobile accommodation. .

SLEEPING
A very important item for your camping experience in the forest is the sleeping bag. Camping in the forest can be cold at night, and the temperature is likely to drop during the night, even during the summer months, so sleeping bags that will keep you protected from sudden or drastic changes in the temperature, is a great idea. The best type of sleeping bag would be one that is well insulated, with a zip to either zip up to keep warm or un-zipped to help keep cool. And what about pillows? A good idea is to bring pillows and sleeping mats, which could act as cushioning support as well as help to retain heat.

COOKING
If you are camping in the forest you will need to plan how you will cook and feed yourself. Some people take their food and cooking equipment with them such as a saucepan, gas stove and enough gas for the trip. It is possible to eat from the saucepan without the need for plates which can increase the weight. In contrast, those who are staying at designated campsite are more likely to have access to electricity, water and even gas. This type of camping which increases your comfort

zone is popularly called *glamping*. The word *glamping* is derived from *glamorous camping,* which is a form of camping that involves accommodation and facilities that are more luxurious than the traditional camping in the wild.

OTHER USEFUL ITEMS

Depending on your type of camping trip you will need to decide what you will prioritise, to avoid taking too much with you. However, a good checklist will probably look like this:

- ✓ Tent, pegs, a mallet, lantern, duct tape
- ✓ Sleeping bag, mat or camp bed with pillow
- ✓ Portable toilet, bin, water supply, gas, or liquid stove
- ✓ Saucepan, cutlery, tin opener, matches or a lighter
- ✓ A first aid kit and relevant medicines, bug spray,
- ✓ Batteries, pocket knife and toilet roll, hand wash

Camping is a key part of many youth organizations around the world, such as Scouts, Boy's Brigade and Girl Guides; used as part of their programme to teach both self-reliance and team building skills to young people. Whichever, method of camping you choose we can agree that it encourages enjoyment of the great outdoors; whether it's with family, friends or grouped organizations. One thing is certain, going Camping provides a great experience amongst nature.

QUESTIONS

1. Give reasons from the passage why camping is considered a popular outdoor activity.
2. Name the benefits of forest camping
3. List 3 concerns people might have when considering a camping trip.
4. What is one of the most important items required for outdoor camping?
5. Which type of camping sites cost less than campsites? And what other benefit might they have?
6. If you choose to camp outdoor or *"wild camping"*, what is the most important item you will need?
7. What does the expression *"designated camping site"* mean?
8. What is the advantage of going to a *"designated camping site?"*
9. Name at least 2 types of mobile accommodation, suitable for going camping with.
10. List at least 3 disadvantages to going forest camping.
11. Describe the type of sleeping bag that would be best for forest camping.
12. Name two things that campers take with them when going forest camping?
13. What is a benefit of eating in a saucepan rather than a plate when camping?
14. What does the term *"glamping"* mean? (Circle the correct answer)
    a. Those who get clamps on their camper vans
    b. Those who wear expensive make-up to look glamorous
    c. Camping sites that have luxurious facilities
    d. A type of mobile camper van

15. Read these Statements and put either **TRUE OR FALSE** in the box

i.	Boys and girls only are allowed	
ii.	Only boys from scouts groups can go camping	
iii.	People of all ages can experience camping	
iv.	Older people who are tough make the best campers	
v.	Camping is not suitable for those who are afraid of the dark	
vi.	Camping is really great for everyone, and all ages	
vii.	Planning is one of the most important requirements for camping	
viii.	Camping outdoors means you can experience nature	
ix.	The temperature can change suddenly when camping	
x.	Not many youth organisations are interested in camping	
xi.	Camping teaches you how to be independent	

16. What important facilities might you find at a designated campsite?
17. Should you take pillows on your camping trip? State **Why** you should or **Why not**?
18. Under the heading, *"Other Useful Items"*, what does the word *"prioritise"* mean?
19. Why would *"Batteries, pocket knife and toilet roll and hand-wash"* be important items to take with you on your camping trip?
20. Which organisations are likely to use camping as a team-building and skills development experience for their members?

WRITING TASK:

Imagine you are on a week's camping trip for the first time, away from home.
Write 3 Diary entries of your camping weekend experience.

"Queen Bess" - an Inspiration!

Reproduced by permission of the Corbis Corporation – Bessie Coleman

If someone asks you how it is that a person can be inspirational, think about the qualities that make them an inspiration to others. Firstly, to be inspirational, you have to offer something valuable or something that motivates people to bring out the best in them. Secondly, you could consider an inspirational person as someone who inspires others to be creative, ambitious and self-driven by a great motivation to succeed. Most of all, an inspirational person is someone who can lead others by being an example, as well as encouraging them to feel they can do something worthwhile too.

Such a person was Bessie Coleman, the first Black American woman to hold an international pilot's licence and fly, against all the odds of living in 19th century America, with parents who were the offspring of slave children.

Bessie Coleman was born on 26th January 1892, in Jacksonville, Florida, where she lived with her two older siblings. Her parents, George and Susan Coleman, were the children of Slaves and because slaves could not be taught to read and write, they were illiterate. This means that they could not teach Bessie themselves. However, this did not stop Bessie from being determined to succeed or to aim for what others would have thought was an impossible dream in her time. Her ambition was to "*amount to something*"; meaning, to become someone who would excel, and to become great, despite the difficulties she and her family encountered.

Her father worked as a labourer and when Bessie was two years old, her family moved from Atlanta, in Texas to another Texan town called Waxahachie. Her parents bought a quarter of an acre land on which they built a house with three rooms and there, two more children were born. However, by the time Bessie was 9 years old, her father left the family home; leaving her mother to look after their five children, single-handedly. Her mother, an ardent church-goer and supporter, worked hard to raise her 5 children.

This made it difficult for Bessie to attend school, as she would often have to look after her younger siblings while her mother and her older siblings, two brothers, went out to work to help maintain their family.

Bessie's education was limited to the age of 13 years old or Year 9; which is the eighth grade in the US. Her school had just one room and often it had to close its doors, when the children were either absent, looking after siblings or had to help their families harvest cotton in the fields.

But despite the difficulties, Bessie attended school when she could and was able to read aloud to her siblings and mother at night. After finishing school at the age of 13 years, she worked in a laundry as a laundress and this enabled her to earn money to help her mother with the family expenses. Bessie was driven by her determination to succeed and this helped her to plan a strategy for advancing in her life. She was able to save some of her wages from her laundry job until 1910, when she decided to leave Texas for another State in search of higher education.

She moved to Oklahoma where she attended Langston University, but unfortunately had to cut this stage of her progress short, because she had run out of money after the first year, and consequently had to leave the University. Bessie went back to Waxahachie, where she worked again as a Laundress for 4 years and in 1915 she moved to Chicago Illinois to live with Walter, her older brother. Her passion to succeed drove her ambition to "*amount to something*", so within months of moving to Chicago, she became a Manicurist and was able to secure a small place of her own. These were temporary positions to help her plan for her long-term ambitions. Bessie did not deviate from her mission to succeed, so in 1920, she set her dream-goal; to become a pilot.

Bessie was tireless in seeking opportunities to achieve her ambition and expressed her determination to fly, among influential friends in Southern Chicago's Black community. One person in particular, Robert Abbott, a publisher of America's largest Black American weekly, the *Chicago Defender*, sponsored Bessie and advised her to go to France, where he regarded the world's leaders in aviation were. There it was suggested she would learn without the racist setbacks that were in America. Additionally, there were no Black pilots in the area, and no white pilot was willing to teach Bessie how to fly. Her sponsor's view was that she would be better supported in France, where she would be able to learn to fly.

So at the age of 28 years, Bessie Coleman set off to France, where she completed flight training in one of France's best Aviation school. On completion of her training on 15th June 1921, Bessie was awarded *her Fédération Aéronautique Internationale* (FAI), which is an international pilot's licence to fly. Bessie achieved her dream goal and once in France, she was able to travel around Europe, gaining as much flying experience as she could, in order to participate in air shows.

Bessie Coleman had surprised the world, having achieved her goals against a background of many difficulties. Therefore, her success and inspiration became interesting to the media. After travelling back to the US in 1922, American media Reporters were fascinated by Bessie's achievements and she was able to outline her life plans for introducing aviation technology to the black community via talks in schools, churches, and theatres. Among her goals was her ambition to set up a school for pilots of any race. This was inspirational. Bessie was articulate and wasted no time in using her knowledge and achievements to create wide publicity and generate huge audiences. Soon she became known as "*Queen Bess*", by the Black American press.

Bessie Coleman's ambition seemed to have no limits as she expanded her strategic goals to levels that many from her race could not reach. In 1923 Bessie bought a small plane but this crashed on her first scheduled West Coast air show. Luckily, she escaped with injuries that kept her in hospital for three months. Her plane was destroyed. This did not stop Bessie Coleman, she soon recovered and after returning to Chicago from hospital, it took her another eighteen months to find backers who would support her financially, in a series of scheduled air shows in Texas.

There were many successful flights and theatre appearances during the summer of 1925 and this, as well as her fame, generated enough income to enable Bessie to purchase another plane. This was part of her strategic plan to gain the money to set up her own school for pilots; a goal which never wavered.

A year later, Bessie travelled by train from Orlando, Florida; to give a benefit exhibition at the Jacksonville Negro Welfare League, planned for 1st May 1926. A day before the show, Bessie and her pilot William D Willis went on a practice reconnaissance in order to survey the area that she would be flying over, with a parachute jump. Bessie's plane was old, worn and poorly maintained. This was evident by the fact that they had to make at least three forced landings on their journey.

But Bessie wanted to perfect her planned performance for the next day, so she sat in the cockpit, in the seat next to Willis. From there, she could bend over to check out the best flight advantages to her program for the next day. However, Bessie unfastened her seat-belt because she wanted to lean over the edge of the plane whilst looking out. As a result, the plane dived then flipped over. This caused Bessie to fall out from her plane at an altitude of 1,000 feet, then the plane with Willis crashed a few moments later. Both were killed.

Bessie Coleman died, on May 1st 1926. She was only 34 years of age but had already become a great inspiration to people at home in the US and around the world, as someone who had overcome great adversities to achieve her goals and ambitions, despite all the odds. Bessie Coleman was the first woman of Black American and the first of Native American descent, to hold a pilot's licence.

Bessie had three funerals which were attended by thousands in cities such as Jacksonville, Orlando, and Chicago. She was buried at Chicago's Lincoln Cemetery and in the years following her death, she achieved recognition as a hero of early aviation.

QUESTIONS

1. Why is Bessie Colman regarded as an inspirational person?
    a. She was the tallest girl in her class in school
    b. She was determined to succeed but only worked for a little while
    c. Bessie's record as a Black Pilot is unique in America and internationally
    d. Bessie was born as a slave and could fly at an early age

2. Why couldn't Bessie's parents teach her?
    a. They were too busy teaching other children
    b. They were slaves and could not read
    c. Bessie was too busy at school
    d. Her parents spent all their time with friends

3. The word illiterate means:-
    a. Full of bright light
    b. Clever and bold
    c. Not able to read or write
    d. Doing a little flying when there's time

4. What was Bessie's life ambition?
    a. To be an air hostess
    b. To be plane engineer
    c. To be someone who was great

d. To become a teacher

5. Put a Tick in the boxes with correct statements

i.	Bessie went to school until she was 13 years	
ii.	Her parents had a school of their own	
iii.	Bessie's parents were children of slaves	
iv.	The Colemans were a rich family who could help Bessie	
v.	Bessie's younger siblings needed looking after at home	
vi.	Her father left the family when Bessie was very young	
vii.	The Coleman family once lived in Washington DC	
viii.	Coleman's pilot licence only allowed her to fly in the USA	
ix.	Bessie's mother brought up 5 children all by herself	
x.	Bessie's school was sometimes closed as the children had to work in the fields or help at home	

6. Describe Bessie Colman's family home in Waxahachie.

7. What does the word *"ardent"* in paragraph 4 mean?

8. How did working as a laundress benefit Bessie and her family?
    a. The family were able to wash their clothes for free
    b. It enabled Bessie to save money and support her mother
    c. Bessie built a house using the money she got as a laundress
    d. Bessie wanted to see her friends as they passed by

9. After living in Texas Bessie left that State to search for education and moved to:
    a. New York
    b. Florida
    c. Oklahoma
    d. Canada

10. Bessie's time at Langston University lasted for
    a. 8 years
    b. 2 years
    c. 15 years
    d. 1 year

11. Why did Bessie had to leave Langston University
    a. The teachers were cross with her
    b. She failed her exams
    c. She ran out of money
    d. She god bored with the University

12. Make a list of jobs Bessie Coleman did, apart from being a pilot.

13. What does the word *"tireless"* mean and how is it a suitable description of Bessie's attitude to work?

14. Who was Robert Abbott and how was he important in Bessie Coleman's life?

15. What reasons did he give Bessie for moving to France?

15. When did Bessie Coleman complete her flight training?

16. What qualifications did Bessie achieve?

17. How did Bessie Coleman surprise the world?
    a. She could fly only small planes
    b. She was the first black American to achieve a pilot's licence to fly in 1922
    c. She did not have to try very hard
    d. America had many racial problems but they did not affect Bessie

18. What other ambition did Bessie Coleman have, as well as becoming a pilot?

19. Write **T for TRUE and F for FALSE** for the following statements

i.	Bessie Coleman had no limits in her ambition.	
ii.	She kept her education all to herself, and was selfish	
iii.	She feared competition from others	
iv.	She used her knowledge and experience to gain large audiences	
v.	She was called *Queen Bess* by the White press	
vi.	She injured herself in a plane crash in 1923	
vii.	Bessie took part in many air shows which helped her to save money	
viii.	Bessie's ambition to help the black community was to set up a school for pilots	
ix.	Bessie's plane was brand new and well maintained	
x.	She made three forced landings in a practice before an air-show	
xi.	Bessie was cautious so she never took risky chances	
xii.	During a practice session Bessie leaned over the edge of her plane without her seat belt	
xiii.	Bessie fell out of her plane at an altitude of 1000ft and survived	
xiv.	She was 54 years when she died	
xv.	Bessie inspired people all over the world because she overcame great difficulties but still achieved her ambitions and goals.	
xvi.	Bessie Coleman was the first Black American to hold a pilot's licence	

WRITING TASK:

Write a Magazine Article about someone who inspires you (*either from the past or the present*). Explain in detail how they have influenced you.

BATH: AN ENGLISH HERITAGE

HISTORY

The town of Bath is set in the rolling countryside of southwest England, about an hour and a half from London, with a population of approximately 84,000. There are approximately 5,000 buildings in the city, attractive for their architectural and historic splendour. Bath is famously known for its natural hot springs and 18th-century Georgian architecture. The city's history is unique and today, visiting the town is like visiting an open-air museum.

Bath is the only UK city to be designated as a UNESCO World Heritage Site; meaning that it offers something rather unique to the world. The famous Roman Baths dates back to AD43, are fascinating for visitors of all ages and give a glimpse of how former settlers lived. No trip to Bath is complete without taking the waters. You can relax and unwind in natural hot springs that have been a magnet to visitors for millennia. The place is well-known for its restorative and healing wonders since the time of the Celts and Romans.

SOAKING IN BATH

A highlight of visiting Bath is that you can visit Thermae Bath Spa, a favourite of the Celts and Romans, for revitalising treatments, healing steam rooms and access to 33 degrees Celsius waters of an open-air pool. Be pampered in the larger indoor Minerva Bath, where you can also access steam rooms, an infrared sauna, spa treatments and an ice chamber. There is also the remains of the Temple to Sulis Minerva, hypocaust with its under-floor heating systems, and more hot and cold baths.

ARCHITECTURAL SPLENDOUR

Highlights of the city include architectural masterpieces such as Royal Crescent and the majestic Circus.

The Royal Crescent is an unusual street, with 30 houses, which is laid out in a curve. It was built between 1767 and 1775 and is one of the greatest examples of Georgian architecture in Britain. ***The Circus*** (from Latin '*circus*', which means a ring, oval or circle), is a great example of Georgian architecture. Building (by the architect John Wood, the Elder), began in 1754 and was completed in 1768.

Bath Abbey as we know it today was restored in 1616. This site has been a place of worship for well over a thousand years. You can take a Tower Tour and climb the 212 steps to the top of The Abbey. There you'll enjoy spectacular views of Bath and see right into the surrounding countryside.

SO MUCH MORE TO SEE IN BATH

The Fashion Museum is housed on the lower floor of the Assembly Rooms and is one of the world's greatest museum collections of historic and fashionable dress.

Pulteney Bridge was completed in 1774 in a Palladian style and is one of only four bridges in the world with shops across its full span on both sides.

The Jane Austen Centre the house where Jane Austen herself used to live in the 1800s. The Centre offers a snapshot of life during Regency times and explores how living in Bath affected the Author's life and writing. Many of her most loved works were written there.

LEARN HOW BATH WAS BUILT
The Museum of Bath Architecture is the best place to learn about the city's distinctive Georgian structures. Models and maps of the city reveal how the transformation of the city in the 18th century and its honey-stone coloured buildings was constructed. An interesting point to note is that the flamboyant Georgians were more concerned about the appearance of varying doorways on terraces showing uniform facades. However the same care and attention to appearance was given to the backs of houses which, comparatively, appear to be somewhat haphazard.

EATING OUT
You can eat out in hundreds of restaurants and cosy cafés; serving everything from Michelin-starred gourmet dishes to simple, satisfying street food. Experience how Georgian elegance meets 21st century cosmopolitan styles in Bath. Sample the tantalising gastronomic delights that a fusion of traditional and pioneering styles can give you. Relax in modern cocktail bars and welcoming traditional pubs, or chill out in a rich entertainment scene that embraces comedy, live music and theatre.

ENJOYING THE OUTDOORS IN BATH
Wondering through the streets of the town is like reliving history through the words of its most famous author, Jane Austen, in *Pride and Prejudice*. The city is within easy reach of amazing undulating countryside, where you can walk between golden-stone villages tucked away by green valleys. If you would rather cycle, then you can do so along the Kennet and Avon canal. Be amazed by the honey-coloured Bath stone which has been used extensively in the town's architecture, including at Bath Abbey. Bath is also an ideal base for exploring nearby sites like the photogenic village of Lacock and Stonehenge's mysterious megaliths, Avebury as well as Longleat Safari

Park. Bath is also well known for its year-round programme of special events and festivals.

QUESTIONS

1. Where in England can you find the town of Bath and what is its population?
2. Why do you think Bath has been described as an open-air museum?
3. Who were the former settlers of the Roman Baths, and which date does this begin from?
4. What does the word *"restorative"* in paragraph 2 mean?
5. What treatments did the Celts and Romans use the Thermae Bath Spa for?
6. Name at least 3 things you can find in Minerva Bath.
7. What does the word *"revitalising"* in paragraph 3 mean?
8. Where in Bath can you access infra-red steam rooms?
9. Name one special feature of the Temple of Sulis Minerva.
10. Which street in Bath took 8 years to build and has only 30 houses.
11. I'm interested in old fashion-styles, where would I find a collection of historic fashionable dresses in Bath?
12. Which building in Bath will I need to climb at least 200 steps in order to get to the top of it?
13. What is very unusual about Pulteney Bridge?
14. Bath architects paid more attention to which parts of buildings? *(Circle the correct one).*
    a. the building as a whole
    b. the front door only
    c. the backs of houses
    d. the appearance of doorways and front gardens
15. Make a list of 5 things you can do outdoors in Bath.
16. Give one example of Georgian architecture found in Bath.
17. What does the word *"embrace"* in the *Eating Out* section mean?
18. Who built the Circus in Bath and how long did this architectural splendour take to complete?
19. Which types of cuisine can you sample in Bath?
20. What does the city maps reveal about the construction of the buildings in Bath?

WRITING TASK:

Describe a place you have visited. You could write about a place abroad or in your country, giving as much details as possible.

*In this extract from **A Woman of Destiny: A Calypso Novel (2014),** Joanne, the narrator is a newly arrived immigrant from the Caribbean to Britain in the 1970's. She attends a local Girls' school where she experiences difficulties in understanding her new British cultural environment which impacts on her ability to do her school homework.*

HOMEWORK BLUES

Every teacher admired my passion to soar in my educational endeavours and this was the talk in the staff room. In return, I had secretly vowed never to disappoint them; that is, until I came face-to-face with a piece of homework which shook my confidence somewhat.

"What is a High Tea?" I asked my mum.

I was stuck on that assignment for a whole evening after school. I had combed through the books we had in our "library"; a cupboard filled with 5 shelves of second-hand books – Britannica Encyclopaedias, medical books, showing real pictures of the human body and an assortment of Janet Frazer catalogues. I had dubbed the cupboard "the library" and pretended the books were all mine. Only the Hoover, an unwanted occupant by my standards, lay at the bottom in its box each time it was used and replaced there.

Mum did not know what a High Tea was. My library books, the pride and source of my knowledge thus far, had let me down. Aunty Mary did not know what a High Tea was either, though she had lived in England longer than anyone I had known.
Both she and Uncle Charlie were the only ones I knew; who had been able to buy their own home in England. That was one of the greatest ambitions of Caribbean

nationals in England, and the envy of some; since it accorded them respect, power, rank and a *rite-de-passage* to success apart from book learning.

I had ceded defeat in the homework department with my Cookery teacher, because I had no knowledge of what a High Tea was. The embarrassment was met with a smirk smile and patronising platitudes, but at least no reprimands from Miss Merchant.

The school had become noisier, Miss Hubbard, the Headmistress, had warned us in Assembly one Friday morning, against showing interest in the boys who were beginning to congregate at our school gates. We were not to show any interest for fear of instigating or encouraging this improper behaviour.

The blue-eyed, grey-haired, formal woman had threatened to mete out punishment of a severe kind, if we were caught breaking the rules. Breaking the rules she stressed, included running through the corridors, chewing gum, a habit she abhorred, and fighting of any kind. And on saying so, she deliberately looked in the direction of a known culprit called Jessica; a Grenadian girl, who was constantly in trouble, with a noisy following.

Jessica had been branded a ringleader, and would think nothing of either bashing someone about if they had dared to look too hard at her; worse still, if they were foolish enough to mimic her raw Grenadian accent. But Jessica did not last long at our school. It was rumoured, months later that she had been sent to an *Educationally Sub-Normal school* (ESN), and that was the dreaded kind of place which Caribbean parents, like Aunty Mary, and others had feared the most.
When I had understood the full extent of ESN schools, I felt sorry for Jessica, and more horrified that the standard of schooling in England was so low that the government had created sub-standard schools. I spent many weeks thinking about the fate of others like Jessica, about what Peter had vowed, and the loss of my best friend Emma.

****

High Tea - a meal eaten in the late afternoon or early evening, typically consisting of a cooked dish, cakes, bread and butter, and tea.
ESN School – a school for UK children in the 1970's, who were assessed as having learning difficulties, such as slower learners or those who failed the standard assessment tests for education in mainstream schools. Due to cultural differences, and administering the test inappropriately, most Caribbean migrant children were seen as failing to meet the standard set, so were labelled as *educationally subnormal*. As a result, the children were taken to school by buses to designated ESN schools, very far away from their homes.
Rite-de-passage – is a ritual or ceremony of the passage that occurs when a person leaves one group or stage to enter another.

QUESTIONS

1. What was the narrator's dilemma with her school homework?
2. What does the phrase *"combed through"* in *paragraph 3* mean?
3. What types of books did the girl's home 'library' contain?
4. What figurative language or Part of Speech is *"an unwanted occupant"*?
5. What do we learn about the ambitions of the migrant Caribbean people in the text?
6. Why was it important for the migrants to buy your own home in England?
7. What does the word *"ceded"* in *paragraph 5* mean?
8. Why do you think the migrant Caribbean parents feared having their children sent to ESN schools?
9. How would you describe the Headmistress of the school?
10. How is she similar to or different from your own head teacher?
11. What was Jessica's problem in school?
12. Why were Caribbean children sent to ESN schools?
13. Have you ever had problems with your own homework? How did you deal with it?
14. What was the narrator's relationship with her teachers?
15. Where is the narrator of the text from?
16. How would you describe the narrator's character?
17. Make a list of the types of rules the narrator had in her school.
18. Why didn't the narrator know what a High Tea was?
19. What does it mean to *"mete out punishment"* to someone? (*paragraph 7*)
20. Give the meanings of the following words from *paragraph 5* :
    a. *smirk*
    b. *patronising*
    c. *platitudes*
    d. *reprimands*
    e. *congregate*

WRITING TASK:

Write a Persuasive Argument, in which you discuss the advantages and disadvantages of school homework.

MAN WALKS ON THE MOON!!

One of the most famous space missions from NASA has been the Apollo 11 to the Moon on 20th July 1969. This mission took man to the surface of the moon for the first time in human history.

Apollo was launched from Kennedy Space Centre on July 16th 1969, using a Saturn V rocket loaded with more than 6.5 million pounds of fuel. The astronauts who made that mission were Neil Armstrong and Buzz Aldrin, assisted by Michael Collins who was in control of the command module whilst Armstrong and Aldrin took the lunar module to the surface of the moon, where they walked. It was a triumph for mankind in general but most important it was a tremendous American victory. As Armstrong planted his size 9 1 / left boot on the powdery surface of the moon at 10:56 p.m., he uttered words that have become the most famously quoted statements in history: *"That's one small step for man, a giant leap for mankind."* Later when Aldrin stepped on the moon, he too was astonished when he uttered the words, *"Beautiful, Beautiful, Magnificent desolation!"*

The men had a camera which simultaneously recorded world history as, for the first time man was able to receive back on earth, black and white pictures of the moon close up, where they were greeted with much elation, by those at the Kennedy Space Command Centre.

One of the most important tasks the astronauts had to perform was to mark the US's achievement in becoming the first country to put a man on the moon by planting America's national flag, called the **Stars and Stripes,** onto the lunar surface. The flag was made of nylon, and measured 5ft by 3ft. It took four or five attempts for the two astronauts to plant the flagpole upright in the moon's surface but once they had it positioned securely both men stepped back to salute it.

It was a special moment in mankind's history and the world witnessed when President Nixon, the American President at that time, placed an extraordinary radio call to both Armstrong and Aldrin saying, "I can't tell you how proud we all are of what you done for every American. This has to be the proudest day of our lives." The President continued, "For people all over the world I am sure that they too join with Americans in recognizing what an immense feat this is. Because of what you have done the heavens have become part of man's world . . . "For one priceless moment in the whole history of man," the President continued, "all of the people on this earth are truly one. One in their pride in what you have done, one in prayers that you will return safely to earth."

Armstrong spent a total of two and a half hours on the moon's surface; Aldrin spent slightly less time but they wasted no time in collecting rock samples and moon soil, totalling 44lbs, which they brought back to earth with them. These were later sent to over 140 scientific centres around the Western World to investigate for clues and knowledge about life on the Moon.

Before re-entering their landing craft to head back to earth, the Apollo 11 crew left behind a stainless steel plaque, which was signed by each of the astronauts, as well America's president, which bore the message, "Here men from planet earth first set foot upon the moon, July 1969 AD. We came in peace for all mankind". The astronauts also left behind, on the moon, a disc which contained recorded messages of leaders from 76 nations around the world. In addition, they left mementos on the moon's surface, to honour three Americans and two Russians who had died for the cause of space exploration.

This historic feat was a major triumph that was viewed globally via the magic of television, by an estimated 500 million people, as they witnessed mankind's greatest and most significant adventure of all times.

QUESTIONS

1. **What was the importance of the Apollo 11 moon landing?**
    a. They found life on the moon
    b. Astronauts left some graffiti there
    c. It was the first time men landed there
    d. They landed on the US president's birthday

2. **The Rocket to the moon was launched from**
    a. Cape Kennedy command centre
    b. Fort Lauderdale Command Centre
    c. Kennedy Space Centre
    d. USA Moon landing Centre

3. **Apollo 11 landed on the moon on**
    a. July 16th 1969
    b. July 20th 1969
    c. June 20th 1969
    d. January 16th 1969

4. Which of the names listed below walked on the surface of the moon? *(Circle them)*
    a. Neil Diamond
    b. Buzz Aldrin
    c. Michael Collins
    d. Neil Armstrong

5. What does the word "*elation*" in paragraph 3 mean?
6. Which famous historic words by Neil Armstrong are associated with the Apollo 11 moon landing?
7. Make a list of tasks the astronauts had to perform on the moon.
8. Was it easy to place the "*stars and stripes*" on the moon's surface? *(Support your answer with evidence from the text).*
9. What did Buzz Aldrin say when he stepped on the moon's surface?

10. What do the following words mean?
    a. *Desolation* – paragraph 2
    b. *Simultaneously* – paragraph 3
    c. *Mementos* – paragraph 7
    d. *Triumph* – paragraph 8

11. The American President at the time of Apollo 11 landing was
    a. Abraham Lincoln
    b. Barak Obama
    c. Richard Nixon
    d. John Kennedy

12. *a).* How was the American President able to speak to the astronauts?
    b). List at least 6 comments the US President made to the astronauts.

13. Based on his conversation with the men on the moon, how would you describe the President's feelings on 20th July 1969?

14. What did the men do the moment they managed to secure the US flag on the moon's surface?

15. Circle the correct answers which show what the astronauts collected from the moon.
    a. Little plants and twigs
    b. Samples of different coloured sand
    c. Tiny insects in bottles
    d. Samples of moon rocks and soil

16. Did the astronauts find life on the moon in 1969?

17. Which astronaut spent the longest time on the moon's surface?

18. The astronauts left some things on the moon. What were they? *(Tick the correct answers)*

i.	Knives, forks and spoons	
ii.	Stainless steel plaque	
iii.	America's national flag	
iv.	Samples of world music	
v.	An autographed book from world leaders	
vi.	44lbs of earths soil	
vii.	Children's toys and books	
viii.	Messages from 76 nations around the world	

19. Prior to Apollo 11's landing, how many people, as suggested in the passage, died in space explorations?

20. Which sentence in the text describes the global importance of the Apollo 11 Moon Landing on 20 July 1969?

WRITING TASK:

Imagine you were one of the Apollo 11 Astronauts, **Write a Diary Entry** of your experience on the Moon.

THE FUGITIVE

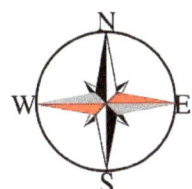

He had managed to escape that hell-hole at last! *"Go west!"* He could hear the echoes of his deceased accomplice in his head, repeating the desperate pleas to take flight for safety during their hasty escape plan.

The night was cold, with freezing air that seemed to slice each warm breath of misty vapours that hissed with each noisy breath out; in his wild and rapid dash to avoid detection. The piercing sound of the warning sirens were long behind him now and his feet seemed to follow a path of their own; robotic and defiant as he trudged through the difficult terrain. His eyes were Gobi marbles, flashing their fearful glances from side to side, as he brushed every hindrance in his bushy path. Branches lashed his face, twigs cracked with anger, as he meandered through the thick undergrowth which popped up like obstacles in his race to the finishing line – safety.

Mizzling rain smeared his head, face, and arms intermittently, as he darted through the unfamiliar woods. Slowly at first, then heavily, the downpour forced him to stop and take shelter under the leafy umbrella of trees for a moment. He patted his pocket hastily, in search of the packet of cigarettes and lighter he had managed to conceal from the guards. They were pinned inside the left- hand pocket of his black track-suit, which was cleverly hidden under his fluorescent orange uniform. He hated this uniform; it had become the sight of loathing for 5 years, so he had wasted no time in discarding the offensive garment with scorn; soon after his escape. This way he could mingle with the general population without tell-tale information that could put him right back to where he had started from.

His hands found the cigarettes. Trembling as he tore the outer packet, he closed his eyes to savour the first moment as he brought the little, thin, white, stick up to his pale lips. He took a deep drag as he inhaled the long-lost sensation of the tobacco into his lungs. In the stillness of the silence, it felt as if it was an eternity since he had smoked a cigarette, so he welcomed this unique privilege, whilst flicking the ash intermittently and breathing slower as he calmed down. Looking forbidding and forlorn, he seemed lost in the spiralling smoke, which mingled with the cold air. He didn't seem to mind the miniscule water droplets as they bathed his face; in fact, he welcomed them.

The beating bongo drum that was his heart earlier, now only tapped slowly to the rhythm of the rise and fall of his chest as he savoured the temporary respite. This was a moment he had visualised during the many years that he was trapped and tortured by his foreign captors. They had concluded that he could not speak their language, when he refused to answer every single one of their questions. This tactic had, in turn, forced him into a world of silence, which was made more torturous over the past five years. Would he be able to speak his own language again? The truth is, he had understood every word they spoke; especially their plan to execute him in secret with a conspiracy that would claim he had committed suicide. That was the moment when his escape plan was hatched. He needed to stay alive. He needed to see his family again. He needed to tell the world his story.

The bongo drum returned to beat louder in his chest and its rising crescendo instilled by fear, jerked him out of his moment's reverie back to reality. He could feel the panic rising in his body as the echo of his friend's voice returned to spur him on, *"Run Charlie, Run! Go West!"* Immediately, his legs became wheels that drove themselves. He didn't mind getting soaked as his body propelled him to his expected place of safety. Beads of sweat mingled with the drizzling rain, and he ran like a hare, being pursued by a fox, in the shadows of the overhanging leafy trees.

QUESTIONS

1. Describe the weather conditions on the night of the narrator's escape.

2. a). What does the word *"fugitive"* mean?
   b). How long had the narrator been a prisoner?

3. Was the narrator's plan to escape made long in advance? (*Give evidence from the text to support your answer*).

4. Find words in the text which mean the following:
   a. A helper or assistance in a crime or wrong-doing
   b. An escaped prisoner
   c. A dead person
   d. Hurriedly

5. a). Why do you think the narrator called the place where he was locked up a *hell-hole*?
   b). What figurative language or figure of speech is the word *"hell-hole?"*

6. How do we know the narrator was held against his will? (*Support your answer from the text*).

7. What does the expression to *"take flight"* mean?

8. a). Which words in paragraph 2 suggests the narrator is moving without his control?
   b). What does this tell us about how he feels on his journey?

9. Find examples of the following in *paragraph 2*
   a. onomatopoeia
   b. personification

10. *"His eyes were Gobi marbles"* is an example of which literary device?

    Tick the correct one

Simile	
Metaphor	
Alliteration	
Personification	

11. What caused the narrator to slow down during his escape?
12. How was the narrator able to later mix with the general public without being detected?

13. Give meanings for the following words from *paragraph 3*:
    a. loathing
    b. discarding
    c. downpour
    d. conceal
    e. intermittently
    f. mizzling
    g. mingle

14. The narrator had not smoked cigarettes for a very long time. Which word in *paragraph 4* suggests this?

15. Which metaphor in *paragraph 5* shows a difference between the fugitive's earlier anxiety and his present feelings?

16. What does the verb *"visualised"* in *paragraph 5* mean?

17. Why did the narrator's captors think he could not speak their language?

18. a). What did the captors plan to do with the narrator?
    b). Give 3 reasons why he did not want to be killed in the way they had planned.

19. Towards the end of the text, what motivated the narrator to start running again?

20. Identify the Simile which tells us how the narrator is making his journey *"West"*.

WRITING TASK:

You are a Journalist and have been asked to interview the Fugitive, for a Broadsheet newspaper. **Write a Magazine Article** in which you give full details about your meeting.

FORESTS IN CRISIS

According to the WWF, (World Wildlife Fund), Forests around the globe, are home to well over half the world's land-based species of plants and animals, as well as  approximately 300 million people. Almost a third of the Earth's surface is covered by forests which also contain all kinds of life. And that's not all, our planet has hidden secrets and each year there are new discoveries of plants, animals and insects that we did not know existed. WWF states that between 2010 and 2013, more than 400 'new' species were found in the Amazon alone! Forests are also providers of food, shelter, medicine, fuel and income for around a billion people. One of the most important features about the forest is that is produces the oxygen that we breathe, and regulates the climate and rainfall patterns around the world.

However, mankind places a huge demand on the forest for wood, paper and agricultural products that has led to crisis in managing our forests. When they are not being turned into wood or paper, a lot of forests, especially in tropical areas, are converted to grow crops like soya for farm animal feed, or palm oil for food and cosmetics.

As a result, there is concern that the forest is becoming unsustainable because too many forests are being damaged or completely destroyed because of our incessant demands. This has led to deforestation at an alarming rate. The scale of loss can be compared to losing approximately one football pitch every two seconds!

On a bigger scale, our planet has already lost nearly 40% of its forests in the last three centuries – and it is said that we lose approximately 33,000 sq km each year - that's roughly five football pitches a minute! The fact is deforestation has produced a crisis not only for the inhabitants within the forests but for our planet as a whole. Some of the biggest threats to forests are caused by the expansion of agricultural land, infrastructure developments, mining and even fire. There is also the problem with Illegal logging, which is one of the most serious threats. Not only is illegal logging thought to be responsible for driving some wildlife towards extinction, but it also it deprives the 300 million people who live in the forests of vital resources and a means of survival.

Additionally, it is not just the loss of wildlife and natural resources that is at stake but cutting down trees is also speeding up the rate of climate changes. Forests play a vital role in the fight against global warming. They do this by absorbing carbon from the air. Therefore if we clear the forests, the carbon they should be absorbing is released as carbon dioxide and other greenhouse gases in to the atmosphere.

WWF's research has identified eleven "deforestation fronts" where the largest concentrations of forest loss are expected to be in the near future. It is estimated that unless there is action to change the present trends, we can expect up to 1.7 million sq km of forest to be destroyed by 2030. Picture this – it's like a forest stretching across Germany, France, Spain and Portugal, all wiped out in just 20 years. Or imagine a forest area that is the size of England being lost each year! It is clear that our forests are in crisis. We have already lost half of the world's natural forests and from what is left only one tenth is protected.

Consequently, countries across the globe are being called on to save the forests by supporting work on forests and woodlands across the world. WWF is working with industries and consumers to promote sustainable uses of the world's forests (from the Amazon rainforest, to forests in East Africa, the Himalayas, India and China), by helping to protect forest communities, wildlife and the global environment. One of WWF's missions is for a trillion trees to be restored, from loss and maintain better protection around the world by 2050, but we all have a role to play too!

QUESTIONS

1. How much of the earth's surface is covered by forests?

2. According to the WWF, forests provide 300 million people with: (*tick the correct answers*)

i	Hidden secrets	
ii	Homes to over half the world's population	
iii	Plants and animals species	
iv	Dangerous animals	
v	Undiscovered insects	
vi	Produces carbon dioxide for humans	
vii	Increases climate and rainfall patterns globally	

3. List at least 5 types of human demands that have led to a crisis in our management of forests?

4. What do you think the world *"converted"* means in *paragraph 2*?

5. What is the scale of loss of forests compared to?

6. Give meanings for the following words from *paragraph 3*

    a. deforestation
    b. incessant
    c. unsustainable

7. What is the yearly loss of forests to our planet in 20years compared to?

8. What are some of the greatest threats to forests? *(Give at least 4 answers)*

9. How much of the forests do we lose per year? *(Circle the correct answer)*

a. 300 million acres
b. 1.7 million sq. Km
c. 33,000 sq km
d. 50% of our forests

10. Which activity increases the rate of wildlife extinction in the forests?

11. Climate change is speeded up because: *(Circle the correct answer)*

    a. It's getting hotter each year
    b. The sea level is increasing
    c. Humans are cutting down trees
    d. New species are discovered yearly

12. In what ways can forests help us deal with global warming?

13. What is described as the most illegal threat to forests?

14. What has WWF's research identified, is a trend for the future of forests?

15. How much of the world's natural forests are actually protected?

16. How is WWF's involvement important in protecting the forests?

17. What do the initials WWF mean?

18. How much forests are estimated to be lost by 2030?

19. What does the text suggest can be done to prevent such losses?

20. According to *paragraph 4*, deforestation is a problem for: *(Circle the correct answer)*

    a. individual countries
    b. people in their homes
    c. those who inhabit the forests
    d. the whole planet
    e. those who produce more pollution

WRITING TASK:

You want to start a Campaign to raise awareness of the crisis in rainforests and have decided to start an After-school Club to get others to join you. **Write a Persuasive Letter** to pupils in your school, asking for their support.

In this extract the narrator is a young girl travelling on her own, for the first time, from a Tropical island to join her parents in England. **From A Woman of Destiny: A Calypso Novel** (2014); p232-235.

A FAREWELL INTO THE UNKNOWN

Now, sitting in this quiet British taxi, I remembered how the Grenadian bus had slanted into a slot beside the other buses outside the Airport building, and the stampede of passengers and families pressed and hurried inside. We had gone into the building swiftly, ushered by quick movements and a seriousness of attitude. Workers, who were already very sweaty, fumbled with heavy luggage, as they carried them towards the door marked **"ENTRANCE"**.

Inside Pearls Airport building, the electric lights overhead seemed intensely bright, in contrast with the dullness of the morning outside. As the swiftness of movements escalated, I had very little time to know what Gran-gran and Aunt Meena and the others were doing at the small Airways Reception. Soon a voice in uniform informed passengers that they should make their way into the waiting LIAT plane. The plane looked smaller on the ground than in the air, separated from us by a glass partition only, within the distance of a stone's throw. Here, the small building which had witnessed the passing of men and women bound for betterment elsewhere seemed awesome to me.

"Have your passports and vaccination papers ready please," announced the steward, and he dispensed with pieces of papers by stamping them loudly, as we walked out of the building into the little waiting plane.

Walking awkwardly and waving nervously, I felt emotionally wrecked inside. My new shoes, dress and handbag felt meaningless to me now, as I walked away from Gran-gran and Aunt Meena. Moving with the flow of the boarding passengers along the path to the plane, made my head swoon, my throat felt dry but my jelly-like legs followed the crowd. There they stood, our deserted families, all the faces we knew and loved, bidding us farewell into the unknown; waving with handkerchiefs and strong resolute faces. Voices called out, *"God be with you!"* It was too late for crying or turning back. The moment of separation had come, negotiated and accepted by all.

The breeze blew cool in the weak morning's sun, lamenting Grenada's loss of sons and daughters to a different clime. Swiftly, once inside the plane, I leaned sideways in my corner seat, waving my handkerchief, straining to look out in the hope that they would recognise me. Passengers had entered and filled the empty seats and surprisingly, the pilot could be seen in our little plane; his back facing us. He sat in front of the controls, as he prepared the whining engine for take-off. The take-off preamble was confusing to me, as I watched the lonely little airport building alongside the plane. In it, I knew Gran-gran and Aunt Meena were feeling wretched inside; perhaps so too were the other families standing outside, witnessing the parting of their dear ones.

Then the little plane shook slightly and the noise of the engine sucking in air rose to a whining scream. It subsided slightly then rose again, noisier than before, as it began to move forward down the runway to the edge of the airfield. I had heard this sound from a distance, throughout my 12 years, and we had daily pretended to chase the iron bird in our childish pranks, waving and shouting, "Come and get me!"

Today, the reality of going away made me sad. The plane turned and circled to its take-off position, it stopped with the view of the shimmering sea ahead. In a few moments, the engines bellowed, rising to a deafening crescendo of power, and then becoming more powerful, it bumped along the runway; racing with the wind, swiftly it left the grassy verges behind. Then purposely, it swooped up from Grenada's soil. It rose evenly above the retreating land below, determined to climb to greater heights above the shimmering sea. It leaned sideways, and then straightened as it left the island, bound for Barbados, before continuing to London Heathrow Airport.

The noise and confusion which continued for a whole day, is now in stark contrast with this quiet English setting. The quiet journey to my home in England was reminiscent of a playing field after an exciting cricket game, when everyone had gone, leaving the quiet, lonely pitch in a sort of anti-climax, until the next play-off.

The English rain had stopped and I tried to catch a quick glimpse of the developing morning. As we progressed to my new home, the morning became more alive with the weak sun which shone in the cloudy sky, inviting people out of their quiet houses, to partake in its glory but in the stillness of the Sunday morning, few people had been enticed out to greet the day.

It was about 10am when the cab stopped outside our orange door. The neighbouring houses had their own coloured front doors; flanked by very little green hedges and square, bricked, front-garden areas. Apart from the yellow of daffodils, the sparse greenery was a reminder of the recent winter; made more pronounced by the half-bare trees alongside the road. They stood like brown giant remains of a blighted holocaust, alone and sad; as was the lonely, quiet surroundings. Mamie Irene paid the cab driver and I followed her as she turned a key into number 21, where, the floral blew wallpaper and the smell of fried bacon felt strange but homely.

QUESTIONS

1. How does the writer describe the atmosphere inside the airport building?

2. What does the word *"stampede"* in *paragraph 1* mean?

3. What event is about to take place in the first 2 paragraphs?
    a. The narrator has just come into the island of Grenada
    b. The narrator is leaving the island of Grenada
    c. The narrator is accompanying someone who is leaving Grenada
    d. The narrator is spotting those who are leaving Grenada

4. What contrast between the inside and outside of Pearls airport with?
    a. It's hotter than outside
    b. It's colder because of the fans
    c. It's very bright and welcoming
    d. It's very dull and boring

5. The narrator describes the building as having *"witnessed the passing of men and women"* What literary devise is the word *"witnessed"* in this phrase?

6. What evidence in the text suggests the narrator was travelling abroad?
    a. She was taking a boat ride
    b. She was going to fly in a helicopter
    c. She had a passport and a bag
    d. She met travellers to the USA

7. How would you describe the emotional impact that the impending journey is having on the narrator?
    a. The narrator is excited to be going abroad
    b. The narrator is feeling quite nervous and sad
    c. The narrator is unsure of where she is going
    d. The narrator is confident to travel on her own

8. Which country is the narrator from and why is travelling abroad seen as a loss?

9. The phrase *"strong resolute faces"* describes the passengers' facial expression. What does that suggest to you?

10. What evidence is there that Pearls Airport is quite small?

11. The narrator is a young person travelling alone because:
    a. Her friends were travelling with her
    b. Her parents had left on the plane before her
    c. Her aunt and grandmother was not accompanying her
    d. Her Nurse was travelling with her to England

12. Where was the plane's final destination once it had left Grenada?

13. How do we know that the narrator's experience was more noisy that its London atmosphere.

14. What is the narrator's journey to her English home compared to?

15. Describe the weather on arriving to her new home.

16. During which season did the narrator arrive in England? (*Give evidence from the text*).

17. What contrasts can you make between the narrator's Grenadian environment and her English setting?

18. The narrator was met at the airport by:
    a. Her friends and family
    b. Her sisters and brothers
    c. Her mother and father
    d. Her mother only

19. On which day of the week did the narrator arrive in England, and what was the weather like?
20. What is the number of the narrator's home in England?

WRITING TASK

Imagine you were the narrator in the text; **write your first letter** back home to Aunt Meena and Gran-Gran about your experience after you left them.

This letter is a response to an advert placed by a TV Programme Director, who is looking for 10 students to take part in a discussion programme on "*violence among teenagers.*" This 15 year old student has written stating why he should be chosen.

Dear Sir,

I am writing to inform you why I should be chosen to take part in your discussion programme.

Firstly, I am a local school campaigner against violence among teenagers and feel quite strongly about both victims and those who use violence to victimise others. Another reason is I have leadership qualities where I have both led and supervised various activities at school; such as rugby, volleyball, basketball and football, with responsibility to maintain peace and calm in the sports. Each opportunity has helped me to mediate between querulous and violent students who have difficulties in controlling their tempers. I have had excellent ways of creating calm and peace in disruptive situations and can only say I have personally learnt a good deal from this.

The next reason I would like to be chosen is, at school, I give children advice on how to keep safe and stay away from peril; both in and out of school. Children I know are keeping safe and taking on board my advice, which is good. The other reason is that I have been in situations where I've personally witnessed violations against some vulnerable youngsters, by youngsters themselves, and have begun to understand why some of them can be extremely cruel, erratic and smug about hurting others. In some cases, they have been victims themselves and have damaged emotions that make them think that it's OK to hurt others. I have also seen in the news how some young people across the nation have suffered from bullying, knife attacks and even death; which have become far too common nowadays!

I strongly believe that young people should be included in discussions about young people's violent behaviour in other to help find solutions for the problems; especially from their perspectives. It is also very important for young people to be vigilant against harassment, and resist being forced to join gangs. Statistics show how gang violence has led to increasing deaths among teenagers in Britain and I am concerned about my own future and that of other young people in our country.

I am passionate to help find solutions to these problems, and would really love to have an opportunity to discuss how we can reduce the rate of violent deaths, incidences with weapons and increasing fear, especially among girls and boys in our society. It is also important that solutions must include responsibility for actions and relevant punishments that are both realistic and effective.

Thank you for taking time to read my letter and I hope you will choose me.

Yours faithfully,

Roger Matthews

QUESTIONS

1. Give 3 reasons that Roger gives in *paragraph 1,* why he should be chosen to take part in the discussion programme.

2. What does the word *"victimise"* in *paragraph 1* mean?

3. Which sporting activities is Roger involved in where he is expected to help students to be peaceful and calm?

4. What do the following words in *paragraph 1* mean:
    a. mediate
    b. querulous
    c. disruptive

5. What has helped Roger to understand those who are cruel and hurt others?

6. Give one reason that Roger suggests why young people become violent?

7. What problems across the country have become commonplace?

8. Why does Roger think young people should be included in discussions about violent behaviour?

9. What does the word *"vigilant"* in *paragraph 4* mean?

10. What important facts does Roger give about deaths among teenagers in Britain?

11. In *paragraph 4* Roger is concerned about;
    a. Young people who are violent and
    b. Young people being forced to join gangs
    c. Young people being bullied
    d. Young people's future and his own

12. What is that Roger wants to do in paragraph 5 to help the violent situations in Britain?

13. What two things does Roger think must be included in the solutions?

14. What do you think makes Roger a good choice for being included in the TV programme?

15. What is the meaning of these words in the text: (*paragraph 3*)
    a. erratic
    b. smug
    c. vulnerable
    d. violations
    e. peril

16. What does Roger mean when he says he *"passionate to help find solutions"*?

17. What does recorded figures show about young teenagers in Britain?

18. What is that might make a violent youngster think that it's alright to be violent?

19. How has helping violent students been beneficial to Roger personally?

20. What important point does Roger make about punishing violent youngsters?

WRITING TASK: Write a **newspaper article** about ***Bullying,*** in which you include different forms of bullying with suggestions about how to deal with the problem.

Ode to Seasons in the Tropics

Under a bright, cerulean, sun-lit sky
The seasons are wet or crispy dry;
Whether seed time or in harvest
There's time to slow down - to rest;
When wet skies appear to soften
Sun-kissed, tropical plants, in this
Two-seasoned, botanical wonderland.

From Rose-mouth to mixed Hibiscus,
And spectacular wild, white, Orchids,
Or multi-coloured Bougainvilleas -
Sighing and playing as they tease
Purple, yellow and violet Allamandas:
And the red Jump-up-and-kiss-me
Winks at spidery yellow Aleanders,
Infused with airborne, aromatic Rose.

Among tree-lined, canopy walkways,
Flamboyant Frangipani and Trumpet Trees
Are flanked by towering Palms on high;
Which bathe when heavy rain cascades
To dance with the flora in this sunny paradise,
Washing luxurious sun-soaked gardens -
Of Jasmine, Jacob's Coat and Desert Rose
And Birds of Paradise suck on nectar sweet,
As they frolic with dancing Flamingo flowers.

Not for me the wicked, wild, winds of winter,
Nor the crispy, chilly, autumnal breezes,
Or the snow-capped, heated, houses;
Surrounded by blankets of powdery, white,
Crunchy snow and freezing, frostbitten, fingers;
These await the sun, which for 6 months has gone,
But will return - to give birth to the coming spring.
No, not for me the glacial snowman, woollen hats,
Or gloves and mittens, ear muffs and knitted scarves;
That is why I bask in my forever summer,
In this two-seasoned botanical wonderland.

By Roselle Thompson

Glossary:
Ode - A kind of poem that is devoted to praising a person, animal, or thing.

QUESTIONS

1. Which types of seasons, does the poet state, are to be found in Tropical countries?
2. Which adjective in the first verse, suggests that there is a lot of sun in this climate?
3. What does the expression *"seed time,"* in verse 1 mean?
4. What type of benefit, in verse 1, does the poet suggest is gained from living in the Tropics?
5. How many types of flowers are mentioned in verse 2?
6. Give at least 2 personifications in verse 2 which describe how the plants behave?
7. Verse 2 is filled with imagery of the colours of the flowers; name at least 5 colours mentioned in this verse.
8. Which plants are to be found along walkways?
9. What does the word *"flora"* in verse 3 mean?
10. What does the rain do to the plants when it falls heavily?
11. What contrast is made with the tropical season, in verse 4?
12. Name three types of flowers in verse 3 that are found in the gardens?
13. What does the word *"frolicking"* mean?
14. Can you identify at least 2 alliterations in verse 3?
15. Winter is portrayed as violent, which adjectives in verse 4 suggest this?
16. What are the differences between the gardens in the wintery climate in verse 4 and the climate in the tropical setting?
17. Which word in verse 3 suggests that the palm trees are tall?
18. What in verse 4, is described as waiting for the sun?
19. Which personification describes what the sun will do when it returns?
20. What does the word *"bask"* in verse 4 mean?

WRITING TASK:

Write a description of your local park or a Special Theme Park that you have visited.

HOLIDAY VILLA FOR RENT

Casa de Caspian is a luxury 2 bedroom, 2 bathroom villa in Faro Park, Playa Blanca in the south-west tip of Lanzarote. It was completed in the spring of 2008 and is situated very close to the coast. There is a car parking space to the side of the property. It is ideal for families who are looking for a really relaxing holiday and offers the tranquillity that is not readily found in the built-up established tourist resorts such as Puerto del Carmen and Costa Teguise.

Fully furnished and equipped to a very high standard, the interior of the villa offers classic Spanish architecture with its combination of granite and marble tiling throughout, providing stunning results and a cool airy feeling. The villa is fitted with charming shutters with integral mosquito nets that guarantee a peaceful night's sleep!

- The main bedroom has a king size bed and is en-suite with bath and shower and the second bedroom has two single beds. Both bedrooms have spacious built-in wardrobes.
- The second bathroom has a large, marble tiled walk-in shower and a safe for your passports and other valuables. There is a hair drier provided for your use.
- The modern kitchen is fully-equipped with dishwasher, fridge-freezer, oven with ceramic hobs, microwave, toaster and kettle, etc. There is also a separate utility room with washing machine and airer.
- The spacious lounge area has two leather settees and hi-fi, Satellite TV - Sky Free view including ITV, DVD and video.
- The electrically heated pool is set in a large sun terrace with four luxurious sun loungers. The outside, shaded dining area has a large teak table overlooking the garden. There is also a teak table overlooking the swimming pool - ideal for relaxing with a lunchtime glass of wine, while keeping a careful eye on the children. There is also a BBQ for your use.
- We have provided a high quality heater for warming up the rooms, if necessary, during the cooler winter months and 2 portable fans for the hottest summer months. A small children's table and chairs is provided for the younger guests, should it be needed, along with a selection of toys and games.
- Any additional baby/young children's equipment can be hired at a small additional charge. The garden has been fully-stocked with beautiful local palm trees, shrubs and flowers.
- A complimentary *'Welcome Pack'* awaits your arrival. We include wine, bread, milk, butter, jam, biscuits and water in the *'Welcome Pack'* and there are containers of tea, coffee and sugar for your use.

FEATURES

2 BEDROOMS: 1 Double Bed, 3 Single Beds, Sleeps a maximum of 5 people.	**OTHER FACILITIES:** ✓ Linen & Towels provided, ✓ Views of mountains, ✓ No smoking, ✓ Heating, ✓ Long-term rent considered
2 BATHROOMS:	
KITCHEN: Oven, Grill, Hob, Freezer, Fridge, Microwave, Washing Machine, Dishwasher	
DINING ROOM: seating for 8 people	**DISTANCE FROM GOLF**: 30kms
LOUNGE: Seating for 6 people	**DISTANCE FROM SHOPS:** 0.15kms
ENTERTAINMENT: CD, Satellite, VHS, DVD	**DISTANCE FROM AIRPORT:** 30kms
OUTSIDE FACILITIES: Own pool, Garden, Parking, Terrace, Sun-beds	**DISTANCE FROM BEACH:** 2kms

RENTAL PERIOD	RENTAL RATE PER WEEK	
Dates available	£'s per Week	€ Euros per week
5 Jan to 4 April	395	514
5 April to 11 April	595	774
5 Jul to 5 Sept.	555	722
6 Sept to 31 Oct.	495	644
1 Nov. To 19 Dec.	395	514
20 Dec. To 2 Jan	595	774

QUESTIONS

1. In which country is Casa de Caspian villa, and when was it completed?
2. What evidence is there in the text to suggest that the villa in Faro Park is not in a busy area?
3. Would the villa suit a group of 6 male and female adults and children? Why not?
4. If you wanted to holiday in busy tourist resorts, which area is suggested in the passage?
5. Find evidence from the text to suggest that the villa is near to the sea.
6. What do the words *"fully furnished"* in *paragraph 2* mean?
7. What type of architecture is found in the inside of the villa?
8. What is the benefit of having granite and marble tiling in the whole villa?
9. What types of entertainment facilities are available for a group of 5 people in the villa ?
10. What does the word *"spacious"* mean?
11. Where in the villa, can you put your passports for safe keeping?
12. How far is the Golf course from the villa and which other place has the same distance?
13. The kitchen is not old-fashioned, what word in the text suggests it is new?
14. Where is the swimming pool, and what kinds of things can you do there?
15. How much would it cost a family of 2 adults and 2 children to rent the villa on 5 to 11 April?
16. What can you expect to find in a "**Welcome Pack**"?
17. How many fans are included in the contents of the villa and why?
18. If you have a baby, can you still stay at Casa De Caspian luxury villa?
19. Where in the villa, would you find beautiful palm trees, shrubs and flowers?
20. What does the following words mean - *"complimentary,"* and *"long-term rent"* mean?

WRITING

Write a **detailed account** of a holiday trip abroad or somewhere, with your family.

WRITING TASKS IN THIS COMPREHENSION BOOK

1. First **write a description** of a winter's day in the park and then add a contrast of the same park, on a summer's day.

2. **Write an imaginative story** entitled: *"They Came at Midnight!"*

3. Do some of your own research on Giant Pandas, then **Write a Speech** for your Year Group, about the threat of extinction of Giant Pandas; together with your own suggestions about what could be done to help the situation.

4. Imagine you were Mel; **write a letter** to your old friend in America, telling her about your life in England, since leaving the USA.

5. Imagine you are on a week's camping trip for the first time, away from home. **Write 3 Diary entries** of your camping weekend experience.

6. **Write a Magazine Article** about someone who inspires you (*either from the past or the present*). Explain in detail how they have influenced you.

7. **Describe a place** you have visited. You could write about a place abroad or in your country, giving as much details as possible.

8. **Write a Persuasive Argument**, in which you discuss the advantages and disadvantages of school homework.

9. Imagine you were one of the Apollo 11 Astronauts, **Write a Diary Entry** of your experience on the Moon.

10. You are a Journalist and have been asked to interview the Fugitive, who managed to escape, for a Broadsheet newspaper. **Write a Magazine Article** in which you give full details about your meeting with him.

11. You want to start a Campaign to raise awareness about the crisis in rainforests and have decided to start an **After-school Club** to get others to join you. **Write a Persuasive Letter** to pupils in your school, asking for their support.

12. Imagine you were the narrator in the text; **write your first letter** back home to Aunt Meena and Gran-Gran about your experience since you left them.

13. Write a **newspaper article** about *Bullying,* in which you include different forms of bullying, with suggestions about how to deal with the problem.

14. **Write a description** of your local park or a Special Theme Park that you have visited.

15. Write a **detailed account** of a holiday trip abroad or somewhere with your family.

(c) 2019 Roselle Thompson   *Mastering Comprehension Skills*

ANSWERS TO PASSAGES

THE HUNTER AND THE BEAR

1. The bear was known for giving good luck and supernatural powers to any who caught and kept it safe.
2. The older generation of the village believed the bear existed. However no one had seen a white bear, so the younger generation thought the tale was just superstition.
3. A person would benefit from catching the bear by getting supernatural powers and good luck.
4. To prove that he was an awesome hunter and the best in the land, also to claim the fame and fortune from catching the animal.
5. The hunter and his family could buy food, clothing, a better home and also have money.
6. The word is *"generous"*
7. The hunter planned to give the white bear to the king.
8. He was tired and very hungry.
9. He was surprised by the reply.
10. He was used to being disturbed and he was scared.
11. The man's tone of voice was anxious and angry.
12. The man knew the trolls were vicious and difficult to get rid of.
13. The word is *"glee"*.
14. The man paced noisily up and down in his room, he bit his lips and looks out of his window nervously.
15. The word is *"aroma"*.
16. There was no answer for some time after they knocked on the door; they could smell the food and were angry because they were kept waiting.
17. The trolls were tricked into going inside the house then a large net from the ceiling was dropped on them and they were trapped inside it.
18. The meaning of *"predicament"* as used in the text is " *being in a difficult or dangerous situation"*
    (a). List of 8 verbs – *mention, was, shrugged, knocked, swung, yell, relaxed, standing*
    (b). They show that there is a lot of action taking place.
19. It was important to defeat the trolls because if the hunter had failed, they would continue to be very nasty to the man and might even harm him.
20. The ending of the story is satisfying because the trolls were treating the man unfairly and now they would be gone and the man can live in peace.

PANDAS

1. b
2. b
3. d
4. b
5. I, III, IV, V, VII, X
6. c
7. c
8. d
9. b
10. b
11. c
12. c
13. I F II T III T IV F V F VI T VII T VIII T IX T X T
14. b

SPICE ISLAND BEAUTY
1. The Word is *"horseshoe"*
2. The narrator thinks the natural beauty of the Carenage is unique and not seen anywhere. The evidence is *"a place of unrivalled natural beauty."*
3. The word that personifies the houses behaviour is *"hugging"*.
4. The word *"amphitheatre"* in the text means arranged like seats in a theatre, to describe how the buildings are arranged around the pier.
5. *"bobbing and gliding"* describe the movement of the boats on the sea water.
6. The literary device is a metaphor
7. The word *"moored"* means to attach the boats securely to the pier
8. The phrase *"hustle and bustle"* means moving around energetically or hurriedly.
9. White cedar and great heart wood
10. The wood was *"imported"* into the country
11. They built these boats on the beach and they built them to their own personal specification without instruments.
12. The narrator was amazed at the busy scene at the Carenage with its multicoloured boats. She was fascinated by the boat builders in the beautiful natural environment before she finally tasted the local food.
13. The word *"resigning"* in the passage means *finally giving up*
14. The countryside was quieter than the town.
15. The condition of the roads was it was that it had lots of bends, *"winding,"* with holes or *"ruts"*.
16. Glen the driver was driving fast because he was *"travelling quickly"* and the word *"careered"* suggests he was driving at full speed.
17. Two evidence is, *"we accepted the long journey ahead of us"* and they travelled *"from the main town"* across the *"second largest town in the island."*
18. (a). The word *"intermittently"* means *happening at intervals*
    (b). The word *"intermittently"* is an Adverb
19. The word is *"delighted"*
20. The word *"indelible"* in the text means *unforgettable*.
21. The phrase *"by good fortune"* means *"fortunately."*
22. The buildings around the harbour look like seats in a theatre, arranged from higher to lower as it comes close to the water's edge.
23. A promenade is a pier and it winds around the inner harbour.
24. The phrase *"the blue expanse"* means the large area of the ocean.
25. The narrator travelled to Grenada and visited an amazing harbour in the island's capital called Carenage. It is a beautiful area filled with colourful houses that are arranged like chairs in a theatre; from the tallest to the lowest. The narrator spent some time in this harbour admiring the beautifully coloured boats, some of which are built on the beach. The narrator was enthralled by the beauty of the landscape which they felt had no comparison. Having sampled delicious tropical food at the end of the day, they made their way to their hotel which was located in the countryside, a long way from the capital where they were during the day. Driving fast across two main towns, in the dark, they finally arrived back at their hotel exhausted but glad that they now had permanent memories of their visit to Grenada.

THE WILKINSON FAMILY
1. Brooklyn, New York, USA
2. 5 people
3. Grange Park Primary School
4. Mel 9yrs; Reece 10 yrs; Pete 5 years
5. After-school film club, football, karate, swimming
6. Mel does 4 activities
7. By sending texts, emails, chats on *Whats App* and *Snap chat*
8. Mrs. Wilkinson is a Dentist
9. Swimming teacher is Bernie who thinks Mel is a brilliant swimmer.
10. On Tuesdays Reece goes Swimming and attends Boys Scout
11. Go camping

12. A GP (General Practitioner) is a doctor and he/she looks after sick people
13.
    a. Meet and greet people attending the dentist surgery
    b. Write down people's details
    c. Help people to feel confident
    d. Make appointments
14. A Labrador
15. She's Mel's best friend, she has piano and ballet lessons with Mel on Saturdays.
16. Accompanies the Wilkinson family to USA
17. Reece does 5 activities after school
18. Pete attends Film club, football, karate, swimming and Boys Scout activities.
19. New York
20. *Write your own activities*

CAMPING AND THE GREAT OUTDOORS

1. You would have a great opportunity to live amongst nature. You would also experience time away from home.
2. The benefits of camping:
   Forest camping allows you to choose a designated camping site. Also you can sample camping in the wild under tents.
3. 3 concerns people might have about a camping trip: (1). Concern about their tents (2). Concerns about cooking and whether there are enough activities for children.
4. One of the most important items required is a sleeping bag.
5. Tent camping sites often costs less and might allow access by car.
6. A tent
7. It means the area that is selected for camping only.
8. An advantage is you may have the use of a caravan or camper van or other mobile accommodation.
9. A caravan and a campervan.
10. It's harder to sleep, cook and live.
11. The one suitable for camping is the one which is well insulated, with or without a zip.
12. Two things they would take is a tent and a sleeping bag
13. You don't have to carry plates separately; you can use the saucepan as a plate.
14. *Glamping* is a post form of camping because there are more luxuries than traditional forms of camping.
15. (i). False
    (ii). False
    (iii). True
    (iv). False
    (v). True
    (vi). True
    (vii). True
    (viii). True
    (ix). True
    (x). False
    (xi). True
16. A toilet, a bed and also a kitchen.
17. Yes because it would be more comfortable.
18. Decide what it the most important first
19. These are important everyday tools that would help you to survive.
20. The Boy Scouts, Girl Guides and Boys Brigade

QUEEN BESS – AN INSPIRATION!

1. c
2. b
3. c
4. c

5. Put a Tick in the boxes with correct statements

xi.	Bessie went to school until she was 13 years	✓
xii.	Her parents had a school of their own	
xiii.	Bessie's parents were children of slaves	✓
xiv.	The Colemans were a rich family who could help Bessie	
xv.	Bessie's younger siblings needed looking after at home	✓
xvi.	Her father left the family when Bessie was very young	✓
xvii.	The Coleman family once lived in Washington DC	
xviii.	Coleman's pilot licence only allowed her to fly in the USA	
xix.	Bessie's mother brought up 5 children all by herself	✓
xx.	Bessie's school was sometimes closed as the children had to work in the fields or help at home	✓

6. Bessie's house had 3 rooms and the house stood in a quarter acre of land.
7. In the passage the word *"ardent"* means *enthusiastic* or *passionate* about something
8. b
9. c
10. d
11. c
12. Bessie's other jobs were a Laundress and a Manicurist.
13. The word *"Tireless"* means doing something persistently, not getting tired of doing it. Bessie was a hard consistent worker who never gave up.
14. Robert Abbott was a publisher of America's largest Black American weekly who advised Bessie to go to France.
15. That there wouldn't be any racist set-backs in France so he told her to move there.
16. 15th June 1921
17. An international pilot's licence (*Federation Aeronautique Internationale*)
18. b
19. Someone who wanted to excel, be great to set up a school for pilots.
20. Write **T for TRUE and F for FALSE** for the following statements

xvii.	Bessie Coleman had no limits in her ambition.	T
xviii.	She kept her education all to herself, and was selfish	F
xix.	She feared competition from others	F
xx.	She used her knowledge and experience to gain large audiences	T
xxi.	She was called **Queen Bess** by the White press	F
xxii.	She injured herself in a plane crash in 1923	F
xxiii.	Bessie took part in many air shows which helped her to save money	T
xxiv.	Bessie's ambition to help the black community was to set up a school for pilots	T
xxv.	Bessie's plane was brand new and well maintained	F
xxvi.	She made three forced landings in a practice before an air-show	T
xxvii.	Bessie was cautious so she never took risky chances	F
xxviii.	During a practice session Bessie leaned over the edge of her plane without her seat belt	T
xxix.	Bessie fell out of her plane at an altitude of 1000ft and survived	F
xxx.	She was 54 years when she died	F
xxxi.	Bessie inspired people all over the world because she overcame great difficulties but still achieved her ambitions and goals.	T
xxxii.	Bessie Coleman was the first Black American to hold a pilot's licence	T

BATH
1. South West of England
2. The city's history can be seen openly in the outdoors, especially its unique buildings.
3. The former settles of Bath were the Celts and Romans in AD43
4. The word *"restorative"* means to bring back to life, refreshing
5. The Celts and Romans use the Thermae Bath Spa for restoring and healing purposes

6. At least 3 things you can find in Minerva Bath – (1). Access steam rooms (2). Have a sauna (3). Get spa treatments.
7. The word *"revitalising"* means refreshing, giving new life or new feeling to someone.
8. The infra-red steam rooms are in Minerva Bath
9. The Temple of Sulis Minerva has under-floor heating system.
10. The Royal Crescent
11. The Fashion Museum
12. Bath Abbey
13. Pulteney Bridge has shops on both sides of the whole bridge.
14. D
15. Five things you can do outdoors in Bath (1). Eat in lots of restaurants and cafes (2). Cycle (3). Visit festivals (4). Explore nearby sites (5). Visit The Jane Austen Centre
16. The Royal Crescent
17. The word *"embrace"* in the text means willingly accepts
18. John Wood, The Elder, built the Circus in Bath and it took 14 years to build.
19. You can sample a range of Michelin-starred gourmet dishes to street food.
20. The city maps show how the transformation of the city in the 18th century, with its honey-stone coloured buildings, was constructed.

HOMEWORK BLUES
1. She didn't know what a High Tea was.
2. The phrase *"combed through"* means to *look through very carefully*
3. The home library contained encyclopaedias, medical books and catalogues.
4. A metaphor
5. They all wanted to buy their own homes.
6. It was a sign of power and it gave them respect.
7. The word *"ceded"* means to give up, surrender or admit defeat.
8. The Caribbean parents feared their children would not get a good education.
9. The Headmistress was a strict person.
10. *Your own answer here*
11. Jessica's problem was that she was a trouble-maker in school.
12. The children going to ESN schools were not seen as clever.
13. *Your own answer here*
14. The narrator had a very good relationship with her teachers; she respected them and was always willing to please them.
15. The narrator is from the Caribbean.
16. The narrator is a very determined person who wants to succeed.
17. The schools' rules were: Not to encourage boys to the school gates; No running through corridors; No chewing gum and No fighting.
18. The narrator did not know what a High Tea was because she was not used to this meal; it was different from her culture.
19. To *"mete out punishment"* means to give or order punishment, usually physical beating.
20. *smirk* – smile in a silly way that irritates
    patronising – treat someone kindly but at the same time showing they are not that clever.
    platitudes – a remark that's dull or obvious
    reprimand - punishment
    congregate – to gather or form a crowd

MAN WALKS ON THE MOON
1. c
2. c
3. a
4. b
5. The word *"elation"* means *joy, happiness.*
6. The famous words of Neil Armstrong *are "One small step for man, one giant leap for mankind".*

7. The tasks performed on the moon were to plant a flag and take pictures.
8. No. Because it took the 2 men 4 or 5 attempts to place the flag on the moon.
9. Buzz Aldrin said, *"Beautiful, beautiful, Magnificent desolation!"* when he stepped on the moon.
10. The meanings are:
    (a). *desolation* – barren with nothing growing
    (b). *simultaneously* – happening at the same time
    (c). *mementos* – items that helps a person to remember an event or happening
    (d). *triumph* - victory
11. C
12. (a). The American President spoke to the astronauts via a radio.
    (b). Six comments made by the American Presidents were:
     - ✓ *I can't tell you how proud we all are of what you done for every American.*
     - ✓ *This has to be the proudest day of our lives*
     - ✓ *For people all over the world I am sure that they too join with Americans in recognizing what an immense feat this is.*
     - ✓ *Because of what you have done the heavens have become part of man's world*
     - ✓ *For one priceless moment in the whole history of man, all of the people of this earth are truly one.*
     - ✓ *One in their pride in what you have one, one in prayers that you will return safely to earth*
13. The President was extremely happy, full of joy and proud.
14. Once they men secured the US flag on the moon, they saluted it.
15. D
16. No. They did not find life on the moon.
17. Neil Armstrong spent the longest time on the moon's surface.
18.

ix.	Knives, forks and spoons	
x.	Stainless steel plaque	✓
xi.	America's national flag	✓
xii.	Samples of world music	
xiii.	An autographed book from world leaders	
xiv.	44lbs of earths soil	
xv.	Children's toys and books	
xvi.	Messages from 76 nations around the world	✓

19. Three Americans and two Russians died in space explorations.
20. *"This historic feat was a major triumph that was viewed globally via the magic of television, by an estimated 500 million people, as they witnessed mankind's greatest and most significant adventure of all times."*

THE FUGITIVE
1. The weather condition was cold with freezing air.
2. (a). the word *"fugitive"* means an escaped prisoner.
   (b). the narrator had been a prisoner for 5 years
3. No. The plan to escape was *"a hasty escape plan."*
4. (a). *accomplice*
   (b). *fugitive*
   (c). *deceased*
   (d). *hasty*
5. (a). It was a disgusting place to live in.
   (b). Metaphor
6. He was trapped and tortured by foreign captors.
7. *"Take flight"* means to *run away fast*
8. (a). The word is *"robotic"*
   (b). He feels he just to run without knowing where he was going.
9. (a). Onomatopoeia - *twigs cracked*
   (b). Personification - *His eyes flashed their fearful glances*

10. **Tick the correct one**

Simile	
Metaphor	✓
Alliteration	
Personification	

11. The heavy rain forced him to stop and take shelter.
12. He got rid of his prison uniform.
13.

A	hating
B	getting rid of something
C	heavy rain
D	hide
E	at intervals
F	fine rain falling
G	mixed

14. The word is *"long-lost"*
15. The beating bongo drum that was his heart now only tapped slowly.
16. The word *"visualised"* means to *form a picture in his mind*.
17. They thought he could not speak their language because he refused to talk to them.
18. (a). They planned to execute him in secret
    (b). He needed to stay alive, to see his family and tell the world his story.
19. The echo of his friend's voice motivated him.
20. The Simile is *"running like a hare"*.

FORESTS IN CRISIS
1. Almost one third of the earth's surface is covered by forests.
2. (ii)
3. Human demands are: expanding agricultural land; Infrastructure developments; Mining; Fire and illegal logging.
4. The word *"converted"* in the text means *to change something into a different use*
5. The scale of loss of forests is compared to losing a football pitch every 2 seconds
6. The meaning of: (a). *deforestation* – clear out trees from the forest; (b). *Incessant* – continually; (c). *Unsustainable* – can't be maintained or kept.
7. The yearly lost to our planet in 20 years time will be like losing forests the size of England each year.
8. Some of the greatest threats to forests are: cutting trees for paper; converting forests for growing soya; converting forests for making palm oil and cosmetics.
9. C
10. Illegal logging
11. C
12. Forests help us by absorbing carbon from the air.
13. The most illegal treat to the forest is illegal logging.
14. The WWF's research identified deforestation fronts as a future trend.
15. Only one tenth of the world's natural forests are protected.
16. The WWF do research to identify problems and threats to the forests.
17. *WWF* means World Wildlife Fund.
18. At least 1.7 million sq km forests are estimated to be lost by 2030.
19. The text suggests we can help protect the forest communities; plant trees to prevent los and protect the forests; work with industries and consumers to promote sustainable uses of the forests and support their work to save the forests.
20. D

A FAREWELL INTO THE UNKNOWN
1. It was bright with quick movements and serious looking people.
2. The word *"stampede"* means a huge crowd or group of people charging or rushing along.
3. b
4. c
5. The literary device is *personification*
6. C
7. B
8. The narrator's country is from Grenada, and the loss is that she is leaving the country and the people she loves - her Gran and Aunt again, who will not see her again.
9. They were determined, brave but sad.
10. Pearls Airport is small because the plane was only separated from the passengers by a glass partition.
11. C
12. The final destination was England
13. The journey to her home was quiet, compared with the noise and confusion she experienced throughout the day.
14. The narrator's journey was compared to the silent atmosphere after a cricket match.
15. The weather on arriving was raining and the sky was cloudy.
16. The season was spring because there were daffodils and not a lot of greenery. Also winter was recent.
17. The Grenadian environment is sunny and the English setting is a quiet, lonely and sad environment.
18. D
19. The narrator arrived on a Sunday and it was cloudy and raining.
20. The lived at No. 21.

LETTER WRITING
1. He is against violence that teenagers do; he has leadership qualities and he can mediate between badly behaving and violent students.
2. To *"victimise"* is to push someone around or selected them in order to treat them unfairly.
3. Roger is involved in netball, volleyball, basketball and football.
4. (a). *mediate* – to referee
   (b). *querulous* – complaining in a grumpy or bad tempered way
   (c). *disruptive* – interfering or disrupting
5. Roger had been bullied in the past.
6. Their emotions are damaged so this makes them think it's OK to hurt others.
7. Problems that are common in the country are bullying, knife attacks and even death.
8. Roger thinks young people should be involved so that they can help find solutions for the problems.
9. The word *"vigilant"* means to be cautious; be on the alert or watchful.
10. Gang violence has led to increasing deaths among teenagers in Britain.
11. D
12. To help violent situations in Britain Roger wants people to be responsible for their actions and that they should be given realistic and effective punishments.
13. Solutions must include relevant punishments and responsibility.
14. Roger is a good choice because he stands up for what is right, and fights for victims.
15. *erratic* – unpredictable or changeable
    smug – self-satisfied, pleased with yourself, self pride
    vulnerable – unprotected and exposed to harm, being an easy target
    violations – abuse or assault
    peril - danger
16. The phrase *"passionate to help find solutions"* means *eager and ready to solve problems*.
17. The recorded figures show that violence has led to an increase in deaths.
18. The violent teenager might have been hurt before.
19. Helping violent students has benefited Roger because he can use his experience to help them solve their problems.
20. Roger thinks punishing youngsters should be realistic and effective.

ODE TO SEASONS IN THE TROPICS
1. The poet describes the seasons as either *"wet"* or *"crispy dry"*.
2. The word is either *"sun-lit or "sun-kissed"*
3. The expression *"seed time"* means the *time to plant crops*
4. One benefit mentioned in verse 1 is the time to slow down and rest.
5. There are 8 types of flowers.
6. Two personifications in verse 2 are: *"jump-up-and-kiss-me winks"* and *"bougainvilleas sigh and plays as they tease"*.
7. 5 colours of flowers are mentioned in verse 2 – white, purple, yellow, violet, red
8. Flamboyant, Frangipani and Trumpet Trees, Palms are found along walkways.
9. *Flora* means the plants and flowers in the island
10. The rain *"softens"* (verse 1) and *"bathes"* (verse 3) the plants when it falls heavily.
11. The contrast is made with winter.
12. Jasmine, Jacob's Coat and Desert Rose are 3 types of flowers found in the gardens.
13. The word *"frolicking"* means happily skipping and jumping in a playful way.
14. Flamingo flowers and Trumpet Trees are 2 alliterations in verse 3.
15. The 4 adjectives which suggest that winter is violent in verse 4 are *"wild" and "wicked"*.
16. The differences are that it cold and freezing in winter and hot in the tropical setting.
17. The word *"towering",* in verse 3 suggests the palm trees are tall.
18. In verse 4 *"frost bitten fingers and snow capped homes"* are waiting for the sun.
19. The personification that describes what the sun will do when it returns is *"give birth to the coming spring"*.
20. The word *"bask"* means lazily lying and enjoying the sunny weather.

HOLIDAY VILLA FOR RENT
1. Casa de Caspian villa is in Playa Blanca in the south-west tip of Lanzarote. It was completed in Spring 2006.
2. It is very close to a coast and the tranquillity is not readily found in the built-up established tourist resorts such as Peurto del Carmen and Costa Teguise.
3. No, because it can only hold 5 people.
4. Peurto del Carmen and Costa Teguise are in busy tourist areas.
5. It is very close to the coast and the tranquillity is not readily found in the built-up tourist resorts.
6. The words *fully furnished* means it is full of furniture.
7. The interior of the villa has classic Spanish architecture.
8. It provides a stunning look and gives a cool airy feeling.
9. The entertainment facilities are CD, Satellite, VHS, and DVD.
10. The word *"spacious"* means that there is a lot of space.
11. In the second bathroom there is a safe for your passports and other valuables.
12. It is 30Kms away and so is the airport.
13. The word *"modern"* suggests the kitchen is new.
14. It is outside in a large sun terrace and you can relax, keep an eye on children or have a BBQ there.
15. It would cost a family of 2 adults and 2 children £595 or €774 (Euros).
16. The *Welcome Pack* has wine, bread, milk, butter, jam, biscuits and water, as well as tea, coffee and sugar.
17. There are 2 portable fans.
18. Yes you can.
19. In the garden
20. *Complimentary* – something that's given freely
    Long-term rent – you can rent it for a long time

Certificate of Achievement

This *Phoenix Certificate* is presented to

....

For successfully completing

MASTERING COMPREHENSION SKILLS

Score Achieved ☐

Comment..
....

Teacher/Parent Signature...

Date...

(c) 2019 Roselle Thompson   *Mastering Comprehension Skills*

About the Author

Roselle Thompson B.A Hons, MPhil, FRSA, has over 27 years of experience in teaching and education development in the UK, from nursery to University levels. In addition to her academic lecturing and writing, Roselle has been creating, since 1994, intensive courses in a number of subjects; including English (language and literature), Verbal Reasoning and Public Speaking for children from as young as 5 years old, to GCSE Secondary and A level 6th Form. Roselle also organises extra support Tutorials for Undergraduates struggling in their first year at university. As a Broadcaster and International Speaker, her approach is therefore to make her significantly accumulated skills available to her students for their personal empowerment, development and life-long success.

BOOKS IN THE SERIES, BY THE SAME AUTHOR...............
ENGLISH GRAMMAR: A STUDENT'S COMPANION

This book prepares children for the **11+ independent** and State **grammar schools** as well as the **Key Stage 2 SATs tests** and **Common Entrance** at 13 years. Although there are a variety of grammar books on the market, this book is based on over 27 years of the Author's techniques based on teaching, heading schools and rigorously tested exercises done in both school and tuition classrooms. The book contains a thorough preparation in grammar, and has valuable **exercises for all aspects of foundation English literacy development** to **secondary level** education and **beyond**. **The Book is divided into 6 sections with Learning Targets, Focus and Assessment indicators and 145 Test exercises, with Answers.** Each section includes work which **combines reading and writing skills to meet pupils' learning targets.**

VOCABULARY SKILLS FOR PRACTICAL LEARNING

The Vocabulary book contains over **60 Units** and **60 Unit Tests** which can be used as lessons, **with a total of 600 vocabulary words.** Each Unit presents at least 10 vocabulary words which show their class or part of speech, together with their definition. This is followed by **60 gap-filling worksheet exercises** for you to complete, without looking at the meaning. Each gap-filling exercise helps students to see how these words are used in their contexts and tests the child's knowledge of them. Check out the **39 general knowledge challenges** set throughout the book as well as **16 interesting brain-teasing crossword puzzles!**

SPELLING & WORD POWER SKILLS

The books in the **Spelling & Word-Power Series** cover **3 levels of practice**, arranged from **Starters** (which introduces the structure of words, sounds and rules), **Level 1** (expands knowledge of phonics and increases the level of structuring of words and rules which guide them), **Level 2** and **Level 3** (provides more challenges in exercises and rules. **Rules** are identified and practice is given in exercises that test understanding. **Practice exercises** for you to complete, test your understanding of the rules applied. In this book, to help you spell correctly, there are spelling strategies that look at the certain aspects of the **sound, structure and spelling of words.** Additionally, some **word-hunt challenges** help you to become aware of the origin of words, forcing a closer look at the rules and word formation.

MASTERING COMPREHENSION SKILLS

This book provides a complete package of introduction, revision and practice comprehension passages to help you with preparation for the Key Stage SATSs tests and those preparing for the 11+ independent and State Grammar School, Common Entrance exams at 13+ and preparation for GCSE English Language Paper 1.
The passages cover work in Key Stage Two, Three and Four of the National Curriculum and beyond. **The texts in this book have been carefully selected to be age-appropriate and cover a range of text types.** The format of the questions replicates the Reading and Comprehension components of the tests to help your child become familiar with the exam format and requirements.

Photo Credits & Acknowledgements

The Author and Publisher would like to acknowledge use of photos by courtesy of the following:
Bessie Coleman photo inset, of the Corbis Corporation
Man steps on the Moon – Daily Express Newspaper Archive
Homework Blues – photo credit to Focus Pocus Ltd
Pandas & *Forests in Crisis* – texts adapted from WWF.org.uk
Bath – www.visitbath.co.uk
A Woman of Destiny: A Calypso Novel (2014) by Roselle Thompson
Ode to Seasons in the Tropics from "Rhythms of Life: An Anthology of Modern Poetry," (2019) by Roselle Thompson

Every effort has been made to obtain permission for photo insets used. The author and publisher would be pleased to rectify any errors or omissions in future editions.